THE ENERGY OF PRAYER

The Energy of Prayer

How to Deepen Your Spiritual Practice

THICH NHAT HANH

PARALLAX
PRESS

Berkeley, California

Parallax Press
P.O. Box 7355
Berkeley, California 94707
www.parallax.org

Parallax Press is the publishing division of Unified Buddhist Church, Inc.

This book is taken from talks given by Thich Nhat Hanh between the 7th and
the 13th of March 1996. All the talks were given in Plum Village, France.

Edited by Rachel Neumann • Cover design by Charles Woods.
Text design by Gopa & Ted 2, Inc.

Library of Congress Cataloging-in-Publication Data
Nhât Hanh, Thích.
  The energy of prayer / Thich Nhat Hanh ; [edited by Rachel Neumann].
     p. cm.
  Edited from talks given between the 7th and the 13th of March 1996 in
Plum Village, France.
  Includes bibliographical references and index.
  ISBN 1-888375-55-8 (pbk. : alk. paper)
1. Prayer—Buddhism. 2. Prayer. 3. Meditation—Buddhism. I. Neumann,
Rachel. II. Title.
  BQ5631.N43 2006
  294.3'443—dc22

                                                          2005035710

Table of Contents

Introduction

T HE URGE TO PRAY is universal. We know of no
culture, past or present, in which prayer does not
occur. People pray when they are happy and sad, during celebrations and tragedies, at births and deaths,
during peace and war, in cathedrals and cars, in poverty
and plenty. Prayer, it seems, is in our blood.

Like the cosmic background hum that has filled the
entire universe since its beginning, prayer is a continual
presence on earth, a constant global hum. And like the
background hum of the universe, prayer reminds us of
our origins. For what is prayer but communication with
the Absolute, from whence we arose, with whom we
are connected, and to whom we shall return?

Einstein once said that he understood his theory of
relativity until the mathematicians got hold of it. Sim-
ilarly, I have often thought that I understood prayer

until I read what theologians and philosophers had to say about it. This is one reason I admire this elegant book by Thich Nhat Hanh: its sheer simplicity. For him, prayer is as natural as breathing and walking, and even simpler. Prayer is not just what we do, it is also who we are. In the end, it matters not whether we say "thee," "thou," or "hey you." In prayer, it is the attitude of our heart that counts.

Lord Bertrand Russell said, "One of the symptoms of an approaching nervous breakdown is the belief that one's work is terribly important." I sometimes think that most people who write about prayer are headed to some sort of mental disaster, because they are so serious. They seem to think that a sense of humor is a moral weakness. You will not find that attitude in this book. Instead, prepare for a lightness and joy that are hallmarks of Thich Nhat Hanh's work in the world.

"Serious prayer" has always seemed an oxymoron to me. I prefer instead the idea of sincere prayer. Sincere prayer has room for a light heart, while serious prayer does not. In keeping with this view, the Christian author G. K. Chesterton said, "It is a test of a good religion whether you can make a joke about it." If he is correct, one wonders whether there are any good religions left in the land. Thankfully, some individuals manage to escape the moroseness that has always infected western religions. For example, following a lecture that Barbara, my wife, and I gave to a group of physicians on the role of spirituality in healthcare, a female surgeon said that she wanted to share with us the prayer she always prays before entering the operating room. She raises her hands and prays, "Dear God, these are your hands. Now don't go and embarrass yourself." Beware those who cannot laugh at their own spirituality. Chesterton again: "A good joke is the one ultimate and sacred thing that cannot be criticized."

In my profession of medicine, we have entered a Golden Age of prayer. Prayer has re-entered the hospitals and clinics of the land. In the early 1990s, only three of the 125 medical schools in the United States featured courses in which spirituality was addressed. Currently, around ninety medical schools have courses that examine the correlations between spirituality and health. Medical students are now taught to take spiritual histories from their patients. Scores of studies show that individuals who follow some sort of religious or spiritual path in their life, it appears not to matter which one they choose, live longer on average than those who do not choose a spiritual path, and on average they have a lower incidence of all major diseases. This data has generated great interest in medicine, for how can we physicians not inform patients about something that can help them live longer and be healthier in the process?

But how can physicians respond to these developments? A close friend of mine, a fellow internist, became interested in the evidence favoring prayer and decided he should make prayer a part of his medical practice. How could he do so respectfully and without being intrusive? He devised a three-sentence paragraph that his receptionist handed to everyone who came into his office. It simply said, "I have reviewed the evidence surrounding prayer, and I believe prayer might help you. As your physician, I choose to pray for you. However, if you do not want me to pray for you, sign this sheet and return it to the receptionist, and I will not add you to my prayer list." Over several years, no one signed the sheet.

Philosopher Manly P. Hall once said, "There is a

type of person in whose mind God is always getting mixed up with vitamins." In other words, just as people take vitamins to improve their physical health, people pray in order to live longer and be healthier. If this is all we make of prayer, it becomes little more than the latest tool in our black bag of medical tricks. Prayer is more majestic than that. It is a bridge to the Absolute. If we get a long, healthy life in the bargain, that is a blessing. If we do not, and there have been many God-realized saints and mystics who died young of terrible diseases, we shall have to settle for immortality, for immortality is one of prayer's implications.

Currently, more than 200 controlled experiments in humans, plants, animals, and even microbes suggest that the compassionate, loving prayers and intentions of one individual can affect another individual or object at great distances. These studies paint a picture of human consciousness that is nonlocal, a fancy word for "infinite." Our individual mind appears to be connected with all other minds, no matter how far apart. Individual minds appear to be unbounded — and if unbounded and unlimited, they eventually come together to form a single mind, which our ancestors referred to as the Universal Mind. Therefore, the most significant contribution that prayer makes to our welfare is not the curing of any particular disease, but the realization that we are infinite, eternal, and one. Infinitude, eternality, and oneness are terms we have traditionally attached to the Divine. We thus share qualities with the Absolute, however we name it: the Divine within.

If readers attempt to convert this book into some sort of rigid formula for their lives, they will have missed the author's meaning. In the end, let us honor the eternal mysteries of prayer, for it is mystery, not some imagined formula, that always endures. No one has ever been successful in reducing prayer to a formulaic method that always "works" in some utilitarian sense, although millions have tried. This is not surprising, for the Absolute is ultimately beyond rational knowing. How does prayer work? My favorite explanation is embodied in Sir Arthur Eddington's remark about the Uncertainty Principle in modern physics: "Something unknown is doing we don't know what." Or in Dr. Seuss' comment, "It just happened to happen." It is not a sign of weakness to confess our ignorance of prayer's workings. In medicine, we have often known that something works millennia before we have known how it works.

Thich Nhat Hanh's treatise on prayer points like an arrow to religious tolerance. His views affirm that prayer is universal, belonging to the entire human race and not to specific religions. Like the many experimental studies of prayer and healing intentions, this book shows that no specific tradition has a monopoly on prayer, contrary to the claims we often hear. In a world aflame with religious intolerance, this message is more important than ever before.

Thich Nhat Hanh's vision of prayer is food for the soul. Let us hope that millions partake of it, for on this meal our future may depend.

—Larry Dossey, MD
Author of *The Extraordinary Healing Power of Ordinary Things* and *Healing Words: The Power of Prayer and the Practice of Medicine*

Why Pray?

I COME FROM the Vietnamese Zen Buddhist tradition. In Zen, we are taught to rely on our own power
more than the power of others. This means we have to
take our destiny into our own hands. We can't just
believe and have faith in another person, even if that
other person has the stability and wisdom of the Buddha, or Jesus, or Mohammed.

But if this is so, then what is the role of prayer?
Should we pray or not? And if we do pray, who do we
pray to and what should we pray for?

I live in a retreat center called Plum Village, in
France. Once, two young nuns from Plum Village went
to visit a Catholic convent in another part of France.

When they returned, they said to me, "The sisters
in the convent are able to hand over all responsibility to
Christ. They have complete faith in Christ and entrust

everything to Him. They don't need to do anything. It's a very attractive way of living.

"In Buddhism we have to do everything: we have to practice walking and sitting, we have to pay attention to our breathing. We take our destiny into our own hands and sometimes it makes us feel so tired."

That was over ten years ago, but the sisters' words still lie in my heart. This book is my way of trying to find a response for those two sisters and, at the same time, answer the questions of anyone who frequently wonders about the effectiveness of prayer.

1

Does Prayer Work?

PEOPLE OF ALL FAITHS use some form of prayer or meditation in their spiritual practice, although it can look quite different from the others. A prayer can be a silent meditation or a full chorus of chanting. In some traditions people sit and pray, in others they lie prostrate, kneel, stand, or even dance. Some people pray regularly with devout faith, others pray only as a last-minute plea for help. Yet despite all the different types and possibilities of prayer, the question I am most often asked is: Does prayer work?

Perhaps we believe that if prayer works, then it's all right to pray. The corollary is, if prayer doesn't work, what's the point of praying?

The best way I can answer this question is with a story. There was a six-year-old boy who had a little white mouse as a pet. The mouse wasn't just a pet; he was the boy's dearest friend. One day, the boy and the mouse went into the garden to play, and the mouse ran into a hole in the ground and didn't come back out. The young boy was so sad. He felt that there was no point in living without the mouse. He knelt down, joined his two palms, and prayed fervently for the mouse to come back again. He prayed with all his heart. He prayed as he had seen his mother do, and he mumbled this prayer to God: "I have faith in you, God. I know if you want to, you can bring the mouse back up again."

The child stayed on his knees and prayed with all his sincerity for over two hours. But the mouse didn't come back up. Finally, the boy went back inside.

Throughout his childhood, he would pray whenever something bad happened. And what he prayed for never came true. By the time he was in high school, he no longer had faith in prayer.

The boy, now a teenager, enrolled in a music class at the Catholic high school he attended. An older man with a shaky voice who was quite ill taught the class. The teacher prayed first thing in class every morning.

He prayed for as long as fifteen minutes, which didn't please any of the students very much. His way of praying was not very interesting or appealing. Before the teacher began, he would always ask, "Do any of you have anything you'd like me to pray for?" He would write down whatever they said and then he would begin to pray on everyone's behalf.

Often, the teacher prayed for simple things, such as: "Tomorrow we are going on a picnic, so please give us fine weather and no rain." As far as the young boy was concerned, these fifteen minutes of prayer before class were fifteen minutes of boredom. The boy had absolutely no faith in any of it. Nevertheless, the teacher continued to pray very sincerely every day.

One day, a girl came into class crying inconsolably. She said her parents had just told her that her mother had a brain tumor. She was terrified her mother would die. The teacher listened to her, then stood up and looked around at the class.

"If there is anyone in the class who doesn't want to pray with us, that is fine. Please go out and stand in the corridor because we are going to pray for the mother of this young girl. After we have finished our prayer, I shall have someone go out and call you back in again."

The young boy intended to stand up and go out because he did not have any faith in prayer. But something kept him in his seat, so he stayed and waited. The teacher asked everyone to bow their heads and he began to pray. His prayer was short, but his voice was very powerful. With his head bent, his palms joined, and his eyes closed, he said, "Thank you for healing this girl's mother." That was all he said. Two weeks later, the girl told the class that her mother had recovered. A doctor's scan of her brain revealed no remaining trace of the tumor.

For the young teenager who had long given up on prayer, this restored his faith in prayer's capacity to heal. He began to pray for his music teacher, who was still quite ill. He prayed with his whole heart for the health of his music teacher, but one year later his teacher passed away.

PARALLAX PRESS

Please send in this card to receive a copy of our catalog.
Add your email address to sign up for our monthly newsletter.

Please print

Name _____

Address _____

City _____ State _____ Zip _____

Country _____

Email _____

facebook.com/parallaxpress • parallax.org • twitter.com/parallaxpress

Get the latest news, author updates, and special offers online!

PARALLAX PRESS

P.O. Box 7355

Berkeley, CA 94707

Five Questions about Prayer

Does this story answer the basic question of whether prayer works? Sometimes prayer is successful and sometimes it isn't. Perhaps we need to ask more questions. The second question we might ask is: Why is prayer successful at some times and not at others?

We know that when we want to use our telephone, it needs to have a wire and there has to be electricity in that wire. Prayer works the same way. If our prayer doesn't have the energy of faith, compassion, and love, it is like trying to use a telephone when there is no electricity in the wire. The mere fact that we pray doesn't lead to a result.

Is there a way of praying that would guarantee satisfactory results? If anyone were to have such a method, people would be happy to buy it at a high price, but so far no one has found one.

We don't know why prayer is effective at some times and not others, but out of this question, another arises: If God or whatever power outside ourselves we believe in has already determined that things should be a certain way, then what is the point of praying? Some people of faith would say that if God wills something, then the will of God is already being done. What is the point of praying if everything is already predetermined? If a person at a certain age suffers from cancer, why should we bother to pray for that person's health? Isn't praying a waste of time?

For Buddhists, this same question arises in regard to karma. If someone performed unwholesome actions in the past, and then sometime later he becomes ill, some would say that this is just an example of karma at work; how can our prayer change anything? If our karma is such, then how can the result of our karma be changed? What we call the "will of God" in Christianity is equivalent to what we call the "retribution of karma" in Buddhism.

So if a spiritual being has made matters the way they are, why pray? We could respond with the question, Why not pray? In Buddhism, we have learned that everything is impermanent, which means that everything can change. Today we are in good health and tomorrow we are in ill health. Today we are in ill health and tomorrow our ill health might no longer be here. Everything goes in accord with the law of cause and effect. Therefore if we have a new energy, a new insight, a new faith, we are able to open a new stage in the life of our body and our mind. When we sit down to practice unifying our body and our mind, and we bring our energy of love to our grandmother, to an elder sister, or a younger brother, then we are producing a new energy. That energy immediately opens our heart. When we have the nectar of compassion and have established communication between the one who is praying and the one being prayed to, then the distance between Plum Village, France to Hanoi does not have any meaning. This connection can't be estimated or described in words; time and space cannot present any obstacles.

We and God are not two separate existences; therefore the will of God is also our own will. If we want to change, then God will not stop us from changing. The poet Nguyen Du put it like this:

When necessary, the heavens will not stand in the
    way of humans.
The result of past actions can be lifted,
future causes and conditions can be created.

The real question is, do we want to change or not? Do we want to hold on to the lure of suffering and let our minds wander around in dreams? If in your heart you want to change, then whatever spiritual being you believe in will also be happy for you to change.

Families work the same way; no person is completely separate. If the son or daughter changes, then the father and mother will also change. If the energy arises from the son or daughter and effects a change in them first, then it will also produce a change in the heart of the father and mother some time later. Families are not made up of completely separate entities. Even if God has predisposed things to be a certain way, we can still change because, as the Bible says, "we are children of God" (I John 3:2).

What is the relationship between the creator and the creature? One has the ability to create and the other is what is created. If they are connected to each other then we can talk about them as subject and object. If they are not connected to each other, how can we call them subject and object? The subject that creates is God; the object created is the universe in which we live. Between the subject and the object there is a close relationship, just as there is a close relationship between left and right, night and day, satisfaction and hunger; just as, according to the law of reflection, the perceiver and the perceived have a very close link. When the angle of incidence changes, the angle of reflection will change immediately. What we call the will of God is linked to our own will. That is why the retribution of our past actions can be changed.

Now, bit by bit, a fourth question emerges. If prayer doesn't bring a visible result, is that because our faith is weak? In Matthew 17:20, the Bible says that if your faith is strong then you can move a mountain.[1] At what point can we call our faith sufficient or strong enough? In the case of the young boy who lost his friend the mouse, he began with a very strong faith. He really believed that if God wanted, the mouse would be recovered. If at that point anyone were to ask the boy about his faith, he would say that he had great faith.

---

1 "And He said to them, 'Because of the littleness of your faith; for truly I say to you, if you have faith the size of a mustard seed, you will say to this mountain, 'Move from here to there,' and it will move; and nothing will be impossible to you.'" *The Revised English Bible* (Oxford: Oxford University Press, 1989).

That faith had been impressed on him for many years. Every night he had prayed under his mother's direction. So why when he prayed this time was he not successful? Some might say that when he prayed, he only wanted to satisfy his own desires for a friend, that his love for the mouse was not true love. If a prayer does not have a result, is it because we don't have love in our prayer?

Of course not. But often the result is not the one we were praying for. Often we believe that we have prayed with our whole heart, we have prayed with every cell in our body, with every drop of blood in our veins, and still our prayer is not successful. If we pray for a loved one and that person is at her last breath, how can anyone say that we do not love? We really do. Nevertheless, if we look deeply we shall see that sometimes what we call love is not love directed toward the other person. It is love directed towards oneself because we are afraid of being left alone and we are afraid of losing someone. If we confuse love with fear and loneliness, then is it really love or just desire? We may desire that person should live so that we won't be lonely. This is love, but love directed toward us. Even if we pray wholeheartedly, our prayer may not save our sick friend, but it may change something within ourselves.

And then there is a fifth and final question, the one hovering above the rest: Who is the person to whom we pray? Who is Allah? Who is God? Who is Buddha? Who is the bodhisattva Avalokiteshvara? Who is Our Lady? When we practice looking deeply into this matter of prayer, we find more questions than answers.

Where is the line where one ends and the other begins? For Buddhism, this is possibly the most basic question. If we are able to discover the answer to this question, then there will not be much difficulty in answering the first four questions. In the tradition of Buddhist practice, whenever we join our palms before the object of our respect, we have to look deeply to know who we are and who the person is sitting in front of us before whom we are about to bow down. Above all else, we need to see what the relationship is between the two of us, between one's self and the Buddha, for example.

If you think that the Buddha is a reality wholly separate from yourself with absolutely no relationship to you whatsoever, and that you are standing down here and Buddha is sitting up there, then your prayer or prostration is not real because it is based on a wrong perception, the perception of a separate self. A prostration based on the perception that Buddha has a separate self from your own, and that you have a self separate from the Buddha, can only be called superstition.

When you stand with your palms joined before an image of the Buddha, the World-Honored One, or an image of whomever you pray to, you have to visualize, because that image before you, whether it is made of brass, cement, jade, or diamond, is just a symbol. That statue seems to exist outside of you. But the Buddha is not someone who exists outside of you. We need to be able to visualize our connection.

In Buddhism, a short poem or prayer is called a *gatha*. This is the beginning of the visualization gatha that Buddhists in my tradition use:

The one who bows and the one who is bowed to are both, by nature, empty.

This means that the nature of the Buddha and the nature of living beings are empty. This idea, that the one who bows and the one who is bowed to are both by nature empty, is something that some Christian believers might find very strange to hear; they might even feel shaken by it. How can there be a religion that dares to say to its founder, "You are empty, you do not have a separate self." But "empty" (*sunyata* in Sanskrit) doesn't mean that nothing is there. Empty means, "Does not have a separate reality."

You and the Buddha are not two separate realities. You are in the Buddha and the Buddha is in you. These seeds of understanding may also be in the Christian tradition and in all other religions, but Buddhism expresses this in a very clear, uncomplicated way. The one who bows and the one who receives the bow, both are empty. Neither of us has a separate self. So, in answer to our fifth question, when we pray in Buddhism, we are praying both to ourselves and to what is outside of ourselves; there is no distinction.

If, in truth, we are practicing, then we can see that we also have the same substance of love, mindfulness, and understanding as all the great beings. God and we are of the same substance. Between God and us there is no discrimination, no separation.

The energy of mindfulness is a real energy, and

whenever energy is applied there is a change. For example, the energy of the sun can change life on the planet Earth. Wind is energy and our mindfulness is also an energy that is able to change the situation of the world and of the human species. Therefore when we create the energy of mindfulness, we are able to pray.

Prayer in Buddhism

In Buddhism, there is a phrase "reciting the sutra." A sutra is a teaching of the Buddha. Sometimes we chant on our own, sometimes with a community of fellow practitioners called a Sangha. Sometimes we recite in our heart silently, sometimes out loud. Sometimes we recite with the energy of mindfulness, faith, and compassion. But sometimes we recite like a parrot, aware of the sound but without giving our attention to the meaning of the words.

Why do we chant sutras? First, in order to be in touch with the teachings the Buddha gave us, to be in touch with the Buddha's understanding. Reciting also gives us an opportunity to water the seeds of what is beautiful, good, and fresh in our own consciousness.

Should we call reciting the sutra like this prayer? If we understand the word "prayer" in its deep meaning, that is, prayer that is based in our practice of mindfulness and concentration, we could say that reciting the sutra is also prayer.

Besides reciting the sutras, Buddhists also have chants that can appear very much like prayer. A good example of this is "May the Day Be Well and the Night Be Well."

May the day be well and the night be well.
May the midday hour bring happiness too.
In every minute and every second,
may the day and night be well.
By the blessing of the Triple Gem,
may all things be protected and safe.

May all beings born in each of the four ways
live in a land of purity.
May all in the Three Realms be born upon
    lotus thrones.
May countless wandering souls
realize the three virtuous positions of the
    Bodhisattva Path.

May all living beings, with grace and ease,
fulfill the Bodhisattva Stages.

The countenance of the World-Honored One,
    like the full moon
or like the orb of the sun, shines with the light of
    clarity.
A halo of wisdom spreads in every direction,
enveloping all with love and compassion,
joy and equanimity.

Namo Shakyamunaye Buddhaya
Namo Shakyamunaye Buddhaya
Namo Shakyamunaye Buddhaya[2]

You might call this chant a wish. But the act of reciting or chanting or praying is not just an empty wish if
behind the words of the prayer there is a practice. In
Buddhism, this practice is the practice of mindfulness
and maintaining concentration on the words of the
sutra. The words of this prayer are based on the

2 From the *Plum Village Chanting and Recitation Book* (Berkeley, CA: Parallax Press, 2000), p. 39.

strength we have in ourselves. When we don't have the strength of the practice in us, then there is little or no strength that can come to us from outside.

In another chant, "Offering the Merit in Order to Put an End to Obstacles of Karma," we recite these lines:

We vow to put an end to the three obstacles and
    transform the afflictions.[3]
We vow to realize the wisdom that sees clearly
    things as they are.

May our desire to put an end to these obstacles be
    universally realized.
Through all generations may the bodhisattva path
    be practiced.

To vow to put an end to obstacles and to transform the afflictions is a desire. We bring this desire and direct it toward the Buddha, so the Buddha can help us

3 The three obstacles are: 1) the obstacle of earthly desires; 2) the obstacle of actions (karma); and 3) the obstacle of retribution. Afflictions are our negative mental states that disturb our peace of mind and bring about suffering and misperceptions. They include greed, hatred, and ignorance, which is the root of all the others.

be liberated from afflictions and realize wisdom. But when we recite these lines, we are not just handing this desire over to the Buddha. We are gathering our strength from within and combining it with the strength that lies outside us.

The chant "Your Disciple Bows in Respect" symbolizes the spirit of prayer in Buddhism. It is a prayer which is based on our practice, and which depends on our own strength as well as that outside of us. We know that if the strength inside us does not exist, then the strength outside us also does not exist. Here is a stanza from that chant:

> Your disciple for many lifetimes, many *kalpas*,
> has been caught in the obstacles of
> karma, craving, anger, arrogance, ignorance,
>   confusion, errors,
> and today, thanks to knowing the Buddha,
> has recognized her mistakes
> and sincerely begins anew.[4]

4 A *kalpa* is the Sanskrit term for a world cycle, an endlessly long period of time. It is the basis of Buddhist time reckoning.

These words are a way of looking into the mirror in order to understand the truth about what has happened to us. The practitioner is bringing the light of mindfulness to shine on her own situation. In chanting, we see how in the past we may have been unskillful. Through chanting, and thanks to the light of compassion of the Buddha, we are able to see where we have made mistakes. We are determined that we shall not continue to act in the same way anymore. We vow to avoid unwholesome actions, we vow to do what is wholesome. These words remind us that we, after learning the teachings of the Buddha, can apply those teachings in our own lives.

Here is another chant, which is more of a traditional prayer in Vietnam, known by even small school children:

Relying on the favor of the Buddha
whose compassion will protect us,
may our body not be in ill health
and our mind not be afflicted.

Practice, like prayer, is for the two aspects of life, our body and our mind, to be in good health. Why do we want our body not to be in ill health and our mind not to be afflicted? Not because we want to run after our sensual desires, but so that day after day we can be happy in practicing the wonderful Buddhadharma, so that we may quickly be free of the bonds of birth and death. We practice to realize the clear mind that has insight into the true nature of things and can liberate all species of living beings. This is our great vow.

Praying for Ourselves and Others

Recently, a practitioner came to Plum Village, the retreat center in France where I live. She was very ill with cancer. Sister Chan Khong, one of the nuns at Plum Village and a close friend of mine for many years, talked to this practitioner and learned that the woman's grandmother and grandfather had lived until the ages of ninety-four and ninety-five. So Sister Chan Khong suggested she pray to her grandparents. "Grandfather, grandmother, come and help me." We pray like this because in our own bodies are the bodies of our grandfathers and grandmothers. Our grandparents may have passed on, but their healthy cells are still present in us and we can call on them to come and help us. When we call on our grandparents, we see clearly that they and we are one.

The other evening when I was practicing sitting meditation, I sent my energy to Sister Dam Nguyen, a nun who was very ill, in Hanoi, Vietnam. When we practice compassion, when we meditate with our focus on compassion, then we practice love. This transmission of energy is a form of prayer. Sister Dam Nguyen enjoyed a remarkable recovery; but that is not the only point. When our heart is full of love, then we are creating more love, peace, and joy in the world.

When we send the energy of love and compassion to another person, it doesn't matter if they know we are sending it. The important thing is that the energy is there and the heart of love is there and is being sent out into the world. When love and compassion are present in us, and we send them outward, then that is truly prayer.

In sending love outward, we may notice a change in our own heart. That prayer has begun to have a result inside us. When Sister Dam Nguyen was here in Plum Village, the other nuns looked after her and showed her a great deal of love. All that love and energy is still within her and within each of us. If we return to ourselves and are in touch with that energy, then we have more energy to heal the body and mind of another.

Sometimes we pray for others for their health or happiness. But sometimes we simply pray for others to change. There was a woman in Taipei who suffered greatly because her husband gambled. She was a Buddhist and every day she went to her temple and prayed that her husband would give up gambling. Every day the relationship between herself and her husband was one of great hardship and suffering. She felt she was toiling day and night to take care of the household while he just wasted money and had no regard for his wife and his children. She wasn't asking for money, success, or health. She just prayed for someone to come and save her by somehow persuading her husband to give up gambling.

But if this woman simply continues to go to the temple and pray that her husband stops gambling, is that effective prayer? Buddhism teaches that we need to have a practice to go along with our prayer. In prayer there has to be mindfulness, concentration, insight, loving kindness, and compassion. Anger, blame, jealousy, and spite are not enough. We need the energy of mind-fulness, concentration, understanding, and love to put electric current in the wire. Otherwise, how can the words of our prayer reach the ears of the one to whom we are praying? If the woman could see that she and her husband were closely connected to each other, that her actions and his were connected, she may have some insight into the problem that plagued her.

How do we pray? We pray with our mouth and our thoughts, but that is not enough. We have to pray with our body, speech, and mind and with our daily life. With mindfulness, our body, speech, and mind can become one. In the state of oneness of body, speech, and mind, we can produce the energy of faith and love necessary to change a difficult situation.

Two Elements of Effective Prayer

Effective prayer is made up of many elements, but there are two that seem the most important. The first is to establish a relationship between ourselves and the one we are praying to. It is the equivalent of connecting the electrical wire when we want to communicate by telephone.

Earlier, I asked the question: To whom do we pray? And I answered, the one who prays and the one prayed to are two realities that cannot be separated from each other. This is basic in Buddhism, and I'm quite sure that in every religion there are those who have practiced for a long time and have this understanding. They can see that God is in our heart. God is us and we are God. The entire visualization gatha goes like this:

The one who bows and the one who is bowed to
are both, by nature, empty.
Therefore the communication between us
is inexpressibly perfect.

The first element of an effective method of prayer is the communication between ourselves and the one we are praying to. Because we and the one we are praying to are interconnected, our communication is not dependent on time or space. When we meditate on this, communication is realized straight away and we are linked. At that point, there is electricity in the wire.

We know that when a television station sends its signal up to the telecommunications satellite and it is beamed back down to our television set, a certain amount of time is necessary for the waves to be transmitted through space. But the communication of prayer lies completely outside of space and time. We don't need a satellite. We do not have to wait one or two days for there to be a result; the result is instant. When you make instant coffee, although you call it instant, you have to boil the water, you need time to make your coffee. Only then can you drink the coffee. But in prayer, we do not need to wait any time at all, even an instant.

The second element we need for prayer is energy. We have connected the telephone wire, now we need to send an electric current through it.

In prayer, the electric current is love, mindfulness, and right concentration. Mindfulness is the real presence of our body and our mind. Our body and our mind are directed toward one point, the present moment. If this is lacking, we are not able to pray, no matter what our faith. If you are not present, who is praying?

To pray effectively, our body and mind must dwell peacefully in the present moment. When you have mindfulness, then you have concentration. This is the condition that will lead to *prajña*, the Sanskrit word for insight and transcendent wisdom. Without that, our prayer is just superstition.

2

The Object of Prayer

WE ALL HAVE WISHES and aspirations and these desires are often the motivation for our prayers. We may pray in gratitude or to seek clarity and guidance. Often people pray for themselves first, and then for those they love. We're not generally used to really praying for strangers, and especially not for those people who we feel we hate and those who have made us or our loved ones suffer.

What do most of us want? We want good health. There is very little we can do if our bodies are in pain. Secondly, we want success in whatever we do. Whether we are a monk or a businessperson, we want to succeed. The third thing most people want is good relationships, or love. If our relationships with others are not beautiful, there's no way our life can be happy. So

we pray that the daily contact between others and ourselves will be harmonious. Young and old, from any
country in the world, most of us want these three
things.

Let's begin with health. We all want to be completely
healthy, but perfect health is just an idea. It's not something that can be realized in life. The reason we are still
alive is because we have been in ill health in the past and
our bodies have developed resistance and immunities to
certain diseases. There is no one who has not been
through minor illnesses; we are constantly falling sick,
especially when we are children. Viruses and bacteria
are always threatening a living being. Microscopic organisms are always present in the air, in water, and in
our food. And because we have always been surrounded
and assailed by microscopic organisms, we are able to
produce antibodies that protect and defend us. Because
we have been sick, we're able to protect ourselves and
continue to live.

So don't wish for health without sickness. Without
sickness, there is no health. We have to recognize this
fact and live peacefully and joyfully with the sickness
that we have. If you have a little bit too much gas in

your abdomen, you can still pray. With a pain in your stomach or an ache in your back, you can pray in order to establish peace and joy; this is called practice. The discomfort you have is just an opportunity to be able to practice. If we only pray or meditate when we are in perfect health, we will never be able to produce peace and joy. We have to sign a peace treaty so we can live in peace with our ill health.

Of course, we have to have a minimum state of health to be able to practice successfully. We may have a garden where there are three hundred beautiful trees: pines, cypresses, bodhi trees, willows, apricot, pear, and apple trees. In our garden there may be three or four trees that have died or are not doing as well. But that doesn't mean that our garden is no longer beautiful. Our garden is still alive and well.

Our body is the same way. Are your eyes still good? Are your lungs still good? Are your two feet still able to take you places? Mohammed, the Buddha, and Jesus all had stomachaches sometimes. Sickness and death are part of life.

The second thing people often pray for is success. Everyone wants to be successful. The trader wants to be successful in his trade. The writer wants to be famous so he can sell many books. The filmmaker wants his film to have a wide distribution. Everyone wants to prosper in her chosen profession. Whenever the New Year comes, we wish each other prosperity. But is it certain that that prosperity is an element essential for our happiness? This is a question worth asking. Also, the prosperity of one person may lead to the decline of that of another person. Many things only have a relative value. We feel prosperous because we have more than one person. Yet we will always have more than some and less than others. If our prosperity is only about having more than others, it will not lead to happiness. So when we pray for prosperity, it seems that it makes sense to pray only for what we need to be healthy. We pray for enough food and warmth that we may enjoy the present moment.

So our happiness may not depend on prosperity, but it does depend on our relationships. For happiness can't be present without love. Often we pray for love and harmony between us and the person we love, between us and our family, us and our society. Can we do anything, or pray for anything in order to improve our relationships? And how should we pray? According to what formula?

Prayer as Part of a Spiritual Practice

Even if you don't pray very often, and spiritual practice is not a big part of your life, you may find yourself praying for health, prosperity, and good relationships. For those who become monks, nuns, and for others with a strong spiritual practice, there is another object of prayer. In the Buddhist chant, "The Disciple Touches the Earth in Respect," the goal is put like this:

> To go beyond the cycle of birth and death,
> to realize the unborn and the undying.

Of course people who have devoted their life to spiritual practice also pray for health, success, and harmony, but these things alone are not enough. As you deepen your spiritual practice, you begin to question. You may want to know clearly, Where do I come from? Why am I here? Where shall I go? After death, do I continue to exist or not? Is there any relationship between myself and Buddha, between myself and God? What is the original purpose of my being here? These are the questions, the prayers, of a dedicated spiritual practitioner.

If we are practicing and we only pray for health, success, and good relationships, we are not yet an authentic practitioner. An authentic practitioner has to pray at a deeper level. We have to practice in such a way that in our daily life we are able to have insight into the interdependent nature of all beings. Our greatest desire as spiritual practitioners is to discover the essence of things and to be in touch with this essence. When this satisfaction is there, then whether we have very good health or poor health, we can still be happy. Whether we are successful or not successful in our work, whatever it is, we do not suffer. When our happiness is not dependent on our success or our health, we will be less likely to argue with others or make them suffer. Good relationships will be there quite naturally.

So, how is this kind of prayer different? It is different because of the level of our prayer. When we have been in touch with the ultimate dimension, with nirvana, when we have been in touch with God, then we can accept whatever happens in the here and now. We have already gone to the land of peace and joy and we do not need to suffer. Whether we have another ten years to live or five years to live makes no difference to us. At that point we have changed our way of seeing the world.

If we don't pray and deepen our spiritual practice, we suffer intensely when we don't have what we want in the world. But when we have been in touch with the essence, the suchness of all things, then it doesn't matter if we don't have what we want. Before, if we were not successful in what we wanted, we thought our whole life was a failure. But when we have been in touch with the ultimate dimension, then whether our temple or our practice center burns down, whether people smear our reputation, are jealous of us, or accuse us unjustly, we can still smile and be peaceful and joyful as usual. What we thought to be success, what we thought to be the basis of our happy life, we do not need anymore. Because our happiness is already there in the ultimate dimension, it goes beyond all ideas of success and failure.

When we can see that we and all living beings are of

one and the same nature, how can there be division between us? How can there be lack of harmony? We are one with God, with Buddha, so how can there be any division? The deepest desire of a practitioner is to be in touch with the ultimate dimension. Once we have been in touch with the ultimate dimension then quite naturally our health will get better, we shall be successful in our practice and our helping others, and we shall be able to form a peaceful and joyful community that lives together in harmony. When success doesn't come to us at the level we desire, we still don't see that as suffering.

The prayer of a spiritual practitioner is very deep. The spiritual practitioner understands that our health, our success, and even our relationships with our loved ones are not the most important things. The most important matter for a practitioner is to be able to break through the veil of the material plane in order to enter the ultimate dimension and see the interconnection between us and all other phenomena in the world around us.

When we pray, we have to have wisdom. When most of us pray, we usually want God to do something for us or bestow this or that upon our loved ones. We think that if God were able to do this one thing, then we would be happy. But every one thing is made up of a million pieces. As long as there is birth, there has to be death. Do we have enough wisdom to be able to set up that equilibrium or not? If we do not have that capacity, our prayer could be just a manifestation of our foolishness or our greed. When our understanding of life and our compassion are lacking, we may want to make a list and ask God or Buddha or Allah to follow it. So we have to look deeply so that our prayers consider the whole, and not just the parts.

The Collective Consciousness

When we begin to pray, we may not yet be good at it, but we will already be able to generate some energy. Gradually, as we continue to practice the precepts, concentration, and insight, our prayers will have more force, more power.

How can we have wisdom in our prayers? When the energies of compassion, understanding, and mindfulness are present, wisdom is more likely to arise. We do not change ourselves alone, but we change the collective consciousness. That collective consciousness is the key to all change. Larry Dossey, an American doctor and author of *Healing Words: The Power of Prayer and the Practice of Medicine*, has said that our collective consciousness is not like telecommunications satellite. We don't need to *send* prayers anywhere, because God is omnipresent. There is no need to convert God into some divine telecommunications satellite in the sky. Prayer is unlimited by space or time. What Dossey calls the omnipresent God, Buddhism calls the collective consciousness or the "one mind." This is the store consciousness in which Buddha and we are one.

If there is a change in the individual consciousness, then a change in the collective consciousness will also take place. When there is a change in the collective consciousness, then the situation of the individual can change; the situation of our loved one who is the object of our prayer can change. This is why Buddhists say that everything arises from the mind. Our mind is a creation of the collective consciousness. If we want to have change, we have to return to our mind. Our mind is a center that produces energy. From this powerhouse we call mind, we can change the world. We change it by means of a real energy that we ourselves have created. This is the most effective way of prayer.

In the Buddhist tradition, we know that praying as a community, a Sangha, is stronger than praying as an individual. One of the Buddha's main disciples, Maha-maudgalyayana, knew that his mother was suffering and this caused him great anguish. Buddha taught him how to take refuge in the strength of the prayers of the Sangha. We have the strength of our own aspiration. We too can send our energy to the heart of the Bud-dha. But with a Sangha, whether of two or five or one hundred people like us, when we simultaneously prac-tice sending spiritual energy, then that energy is mag-nified and much more effective.

We pray, but sometimes we may have a situation that is very difficult and we need a stronger energy. The individual energy we can send is already something, but if we have a Sangha that is free and solid then the energy we can send together will certainly be greater. When the whole community prays with us, it can be a significant moment in our lives. We are one of the Sangha who is praying. Our own undivided attention is a key to open the door of the ultimate reality and the undivided attention of our friends in the practice is an even greater key. When a Sangha of one hundred or one thousand people practices purifying the actions of body, speech, and mind, and unifying body and mind to send energy, the energy generated will be very powerful, and will be able to change the situation which we call karma, the causes and effects of our actions.

3

Heart, Body, Spirit

IN BUDDHISM, we know that the one we are praying to lies inside as well as outside of us. Buddha lies in our heart, and God also lies in our heart. It is a mistake to think that God is only outside.

We can draw a letter *A*, symbolizing a person praying, and a letter *B*, symbolizing the one who is the object of our prayer. We can make a circle that represents God. There are two ways of seeing our relationship to this circle. If God is a separate entity, we send our prayers to God and God sends them to the object of our prayer. But we can also put A and B in the same circle. By doing this, we remove one of the layers of wrong perception which comes from the idea that we and Buddha are two things, that we and God are two things.

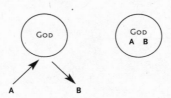

DIAGRAM 1: GOD AND THE ONE WHO IS PRAYED FOR.

The collective consciousness is made up of the individual consciousness and the individual consciousness is made up of the collective consciousness. The two things make each other possible. It's not that one comes first and the other comes later. There is no "above" without "below," there is no "inside" without "outside"; the two things have to be there at the same time. The same is true with "I" and "we": they make each other possible. "This is because that is, that is because this is." This is a teaching of the Buddha.

In Christianity and Judaism, we can call this omnipresent presence "God." God and Buddha are not two different things. We should not allow words and expressions to deceive us. The important thing is that we are able to be in touch with reality. The yellow fruit that you peel is called *chui* in Vietnamese and "banana" in English, but it's the same fruit. Both words point to the same reality.

The Three Keys

Suppose a loved one is suffering or in danger. We need to surround our loved one with wholesome energy so they can be protected. We need help, and that is why we pray. When we pray, we want to be able to touch God, and we can use one of the three keys of Buddhism, which are put together on one key ring and called the Three Dharma Seals. These three keys are impermanence, no-self, and nirvana. They are very wonderful instruments, and wherever we are they can allow us to open the door to many priceless treasures.

All religious traditions have some reference to impermanence. We see clearly that there is nothing that lasts forever. No-self is just another aspect of impermanence. Things are impermanent and changing. Nothing that exists has a separate reality independent of anything else. The person who prays and the one who is prayed to are both empty; neither has a separate self. The same is true of collective consciousness and individual consciousness. The individual consciousness doesn't have a self separate from the collective consciousness.

In the same way, thanks to the understanding of no-self, we can see that *A, B,* and God are not separate realities. If we are not here, then how can we know that God is there? The principle of no-self is a wonderful key because it removes the barriers between our material daily lives and the ultimate spiritual dimension.

The third key is nirvana. What is nirvana? Is nirvana something separate from the world of birth and death in which we are now living? Are nirvana and birth and death two separate realities? Although they are called two different things, if we accept the second key of no-self, we see that they are in fact one reality. It is like waves and water. Waves are different from water, but outside waves there is no water, and outside water there are no waves. Waves and water inter-are. In this material world, we call it the world of birth-and-death, but as far as the essential nature, the ultimate dimension, is concerned, we can call this world "nirvana." If we know how to be deeply in touch with the solid, free, and refreshing nature of birds, trees, people, flowers and all phenomena around us, then through the phenomenal world we can be in touch with the ultimate dimension, the world of nirvana.

The Three Dharma Seals is a Buddhist teaching, but I have used it to understand much about Christianity, Judaism, Islam, and other religions. I have opened numerous doors and been able to discover countless jewels in the treasury of Christian teachings and the teachings of other traditions. The teachings of the Three Dharma Seals are also present in the Bible and the Koran.

Touching God

We need to look deeply to know how to be able to be in touch with God. According to the German-American theologian Paul Tillich, God is the foundation of all that is, the ground of being.

According to that definition, if God is the foundation, then what is being? Being is the creation of God. So, how can we be in touch with God if we're not in touch with what God has created? We can touch God through God's creations. When we pray, we can be in

touch with the ground of being through the phenomenal world.

Shakyamuni Buddha is a phenomenon, a person with
a name, a birth date, a father and a mother, a date of
death. There is a part of the planet Earth where
Shakyamuni was born, lived, practiced, and taught his
disciples. But the essence of Buddha is Buddha nature.
All of us have this awakened nature. In the Lotus Sutra,
the Buddha puts it like this: "All living beings have the
capacity to become Buddha. The essential nature of
living beings is the Buddha nature." When we pray to
the Buddha, we are getting in touch with Buddha
nature. And when we pray to ourselves, we also get in
touch with Buddha nature.

In Vietnam, we also have a custom of praying to
spirits, those who have died and become holy souls.
We also pray to our ancestors and to our parents who
have passed away. We pray because we believe firmly
that when we are in touch with these people, we receive
energy from them that will help us. For thousands of
years in Vietnam, whenever people have had problems,
they have lit incense and prayed to their ancestors.

Prayer of the Heart and Prayer of the Body

You may have heard of the prayer of the heart, but prayer of the body is just as important. When Buddhist or Christian monks and nuns pray, they kneel down, join their palms, and bow their heads. It is essential for prayer that body, speech, and mind are one, and are all truly present. It is not enough to pray with words; effective prayer also takes mental and physical concentration. Perhaps that is why many religions, such as Buddhism, Islam, and the Orthodox Church, include prostrations in prayer. It is a position that diminishes the ego, opens one up, and brings one close to the earth.

Through my own prayer I have discovered that it is as helpful to pray to the living as it is to pray to those who have passed away. The happiness and lucidity of those around us can also add energy to our prayers. Within our circle of friends and family, there are those whom we see as solid, as an inspiration. Thinking of these people can bring more energy into our bodies.

One time, one of my students came to me feeling very sad. I was about to leave on a trip but I suggested: "When I am not there you can come into my room and sit there alone." Sitting in that room, it was as if he was sitting with his teacher, and receiving some of his teacher's energy. This kind of communion is also a form of prayer.

In difficult moments, if our mind is conditioned in the direction of someone in whom we have faith, then we have more energy to overcome life's uncertainties. So we can pray keeping in mind the individuals that inspire us, and we can also pray to our communities. Suppose our family or our group of friends is doing well. They are not doing anything miraculous, but everyone is healthy and appreciating each other. When we go far away and when we feel tired or sad, or we have difficulties, we only need to think about our community and we may feel more energized.

Praying to those who are still with us is not that different from praying to those who have passed away. We know that those who have passed away are still with us. And those who are still alive are also still with us. When someone has died, people think that person is no longer there. But according to the teachings of the Buddha, that person is always there.

There are many stories of people who have been

pronounced dead and then come back to life. That is why in Vietnam we never allow someone who has died to be buried straightaway. We have to wait at least two days, then we put the corpse on the earth to see if the cool vapor from the earth will make the dead person live again. People take a piece of the dead person's clothing, climb on to the roof of the house, stretch it out, and call on the three souls and the nine vital spirits of the dead person to come back, just in case the soul of the dead person might hear and return to take up its place again in the corpse to live. Vietnamese people have the custom of taking every precaution before burying a dead person, because they do not want to make a mistake.

According to the teaching of the Buddha, nothing is born and nothing dies. When our grandfather or grandmother dies, they are no longer with us in the way they used to be. But they could be manifesting themselves in some other way that our eyes are not yet able to recognize. They are always there. So it is still effective to pray to our grandfather and our grandmother. When we know clearly to whom we are praying, that prayer will be more effective. When we pray to those with whom we have been in touch, those we knew when they were alive, then the energy can arise and make us stronger.

All Buddhists have their own experience and their own perceptions of the deeper nature of the Buddha. If you study the life and teachings of the Buddha and apply them to your daily life, you will see their effect. The Buddha is not just someone sitting on an altar, but someone familiar. Seeing someone is not the same as knowing them. Although none of us were alive in the time of the Buddha, we can know him better than someone who was alive at that time. If someone had met the Buddha as he was walking to Vulture Peak, but kept walking without learning anything of the Buddha's life, happiness, or teachings, then although she or he had seen the Buddha directly, that person still would not have had a deep understanding of the Buddha.[5]

Buddha is right here; we don't have to go to the Vulture Peak. We are not deceived by mere outer appearances. For me, Buddha is not just a form or a name,

5 Vulture Peak is the mountain near the town of Rajagriha, in India, where the Buddha sometimes stayed and taught.

Buddha is a reality. I live with the Buddha every day. When eating, I sit with the Buddha. When I walk, I walk with the Buddha. And while I'm giving a Dharma talk, I'm also living with the Buddha.

I wouldn't exchange this essence of the Buddha for a chance to see the outer form of the Buddha. We shouldn't rush and call the travel agency so we can fly to India and climb up the Vulture Peak to see the Buddha. No matter how seductive advertisements might be, they can't deceive us. We have Buddha right here. Whenever we do walking meditation, we can take hold of the hand of the Buddha and walk. That is why in Buddhism we can say, "We enjoy our walk in the ultimate dimension, holding the hand of the Buddha."

We can also be in touch with the bodhisattvas. In Buddhism, bodhisattvas are great beings who walk on this earth and embody compassion and wisdom. In our Sangha there are living bodhisattvas. These bodhisattvas have the capacity to listen to us, to understand us, and can use their strength and their heart to help others. This is something real. Sometimes these bodhisattvas are still very young. We should not look for bodhisattvas up in the sky. Sometimes we are sleeping in the same room as a bodhisattva and we do not even know it. When you have a problem, an anxiety, or you have met some difficulty, that bodhisattva can help you. That bodhisattva made of flesh and bones is your sister or brother in the Sangha. We like to go in search of a bodhisattva in the sky, but maybe we are living under the same roof with three or four bodhisattvas, though we are indifferent to them and do not see their value.

What is a bodhisattva? A bodhisattva is someone who has the energy of understanding, of love, and also the energy of action. When we meet difficulties, when we fall into a dangerous situation, the bodhisattva can come and can rescue us. If you understand "bodhisattva" in that way, then you will see that, in truth, we *do* have living bodhisattvas, bodhisattvas who are living right alongside us in the Sangha. They are practicing with us and making realizations in the practice every day.

People may say that the bodhisattvas in Buddhist scripture do not have a historical reality. We cannot say what day they were born and what day they died. But we do not need a historical reality. For example, we know that the essential nature of the bodhisattva Avalokiteshvara is love, and love is something real in this life.

It doesn't matter whether Avalokiteshvara is a woman or a man, black or white, a child or a politician; if there is love, then the bodhisattva is there. A historian could never take away my faith in Avalokiteshvara, because I know very clearly that love is something real, manifesting itself in many different forms.

In Holland there is a woman named Hebe Kolhbrugge who, during the Second World War, was able to rescue at least 30,000 Jewish people from the Nazi gas chambers. This woman is nothing other than the bodhisattva Avalokiteshvara. This woman is still alive. During the war in Vietnam, she sponsored many children who had lost one or both parents.

I have prayed to the Buddha and the bodhisattvas, to the ancestors, to my father and my mother. Sometimes I even pray to my students, because there are students who have a great deal of energy, stability, freedom, and happiness, and I need to come to them as objects of my prayer. I have also prayed to my community that is present throughout the world, because I need its strength. Whenever I pray, I know that I am in touch with the energy of the one mind through these people.

And if we are praying with the body as well as the

heart and mind, then we can also pray to the pine tree, the moon, and the stars. The pine tree is quite solid, the moon is always there on time, and the stars are always there for us, free and bright. If we can be deeply in touch with the pine tree, we are able to be in touch with the one mind, with God. If touching God means that God is able to transmit energy to us, then the pine tree can also transmit energy to us.

One day in winter, Saint Francis of Assisi was practicing mindful walking and he came upon an almond tree. He stopped before the tree, breathed, and prayed, "Almond tree, tell me about God." And then, quite naturally the almond tree blossomed into flower, even in the biting cold of winter. In the historical dimension, our daily reality, the almond tree does not yet have flowers. But in the world of the ultimate dimension, the almond tree has had flowers for tens of thousands of years. As far as the historical dimension is concerned, the Buddha lived and died and we are not the Buddha. But as far as the ultimate dimension is concerned, we are already Buddha. So being in touch with the almond tree is a way of being in touch with God. You will not find God in an abstract idea. This is something very important. God is here for us through very concrete things.

Sometimes when we pray, we see that the words of the prayer are effective. Sometimes we get a result so strongly, it is as if God is saying "yes." Sometimes we get the reply "not yet," sometimes "maybe," and sometimes "no." That "no" is hard to hear, but know that this is not the refusal of God, of the Buddha, of the bodhisattva, but the energy sent is not yet strong enough to change the situation. We need a few more conditions. Prayer always has a result, but the level of the result varies.

When the answer is "no" it does not necessarily mean that our prayer is ineffective. It may be creating results that we cannot yet see. Often we do not know our true needs, and the collective consciousness knows us better than we know ourselves. For example, say a young woman wants to pass a test at school. She, and her family, may pray a great deal but still she doesn't pass. She may think that her prayer is ineffective. But perhaps there is some reason in that failure. If we fail this time, perhaps the next time we will be more solid, more ready to be successful on our path in life.

In Vietnam, people tell the story of a very intelligent young man who went to take the civil service examination. He did the best of all the candidates, but when the heads of the school were discussing his situation, they said that, although he had done so well in the exam, he was still very young and they were afraid that his ambition was not yet polished enough. So they decided to fail him this time and to pass him the next time the exam was given. From the outside this seems very unjust. But the nation has to form young people to do well in all ways. They need to be accomplished not only in intellect, but in virtuous conduct as well. The heads of the school were acting according to this principle, and trying to polish the ambition of the young candidate. If his will was strong, even though he would have to wait another three years for the next exam, it would not be too late because he was still very young.

People need to have a strong aspiration before they can become a bodhisattva who can liberate beings from suffering or someone skilled in helping the people and the nation. The young man in this case could have raged and complained. He could have given up. But he kept studying. When the young man took the exam three years later, he passed. He then took the imperial court examination and passed that too, and went on to serve his country very well.

When he failed the first time, he may have suffered. He did not know that all this was to help him grow up and do better. It is the same when we pray. We think that we did not receive what we prayed for, but we don't realize that we might have received something else, perhaps something greater or less than what we asked for. Our Buddha nature knows us better than we know ourselves, knows more clearly what is best for us.

The Lord's Prayer: Buddhist and Christian Parallels

The Orthodox Church doctrine states very clearly that every human being has the divine nature of God and shares in the divine goodness of God. This is the same as the Buddhist concept of our Buddha nature. While they may be different on the surface, Christian and Buddhist teachings have much in common.

In Chapter One, we looked at this Buddhist chant, "Your Disciple Bows in Respect":

Your disciple for many lifetimes, many kalpas,
has been caught in the obstacles of
karma, craving, anger, arrogance, ignorance,
    confusion, errors,
and today, thanks to knowing the Buddha,
has recognized her mistakes
and sincerely begins anew.

Now, let's look at the Lord's Prayer, a well-known prayer in Christian traditions.

Our Father in heaven,
hallowed be your name.
Your kingdom come,
your will be done
on Earth as it is in heaven.
Give us today our daily bread
and forgive us our debts
as we have also forgiven our debtors.
Do not lead us into temptation,
but deliver us from evil.[6]

6 *The Revised English Bible* (Oxford: Oxford University Press, 1989).
Matthew 6: 9–13.

If we look deeply, we see that with this prayer we are also practicing to be in touch with the ultimate dimension. What are we looking for? We are looking for something very great. We are not asking God to let the sun shine so that we can have a good picnic. We are not just looking for little peanuts, we are looking for the kingdom of God. Our first aim in prayer is the kingdom of God. Let's look at this prayer line by line.

Our Father in heaven, Hallowed be your name.

In heaven means "not in the historical phenomenal world." Although God is in everything, we can't compare God with creatures that live on Earth, just as we cannot compare water with a wave, because one is the ultimate nature and one is the phenomenon. We can compare one wave with another, but we cannot compare the water with the wave. It is the ultimate nature, and no words can be used to give it a name or describe it. We could call it God, we could call it Allah, we could call it the creator, but these are just ways of naming it. All these expressions and ideas are our unsuccessful attempt to define God. Therefore, whether we say God, or *Dieu* (French), or *Thuong De* (Vietnamese) or Allah, these are just names, and are not strong enough to contain the wonderful reality that is the ultimate dimension.

To be in touch with the wonderful reality of the ultimate dimension, we have to go beyond the name, and only then can we find the true hallowed nature. The *Tao Te Ching* says: "The path that can still be discussed, is not yet the true eternal path. The name that can be called, is not yet the true eternal name."

Hallowed be your name.

This refers to God's name, but in truth, God is not a name that can be called out to as if God is a person just across the street from us. If God is within us and around us, how can we even express this in one name?

Your kingdom come.

The word "kingdom" is translated from the Greek word *basileia*, which has three different meanings. The first meaning is "realm," the land or country of God. This first meaning is from the point of view of the sign. The second meaning is "royalty." It means the nature of the realm, it's kingliness. That realm has the nature of happiness, of eternity, of peace and joy. Royalty is the nature and realm is the sign. Kingdom is the sign, and kingdom-ness the nature. The nature is nirvana, the sign is the sign of no birth and no death. In this we have both the sign and the nature. The third meaning is "reign," the act of ruling, which is the way that realm and life in that realm can be described. Realm belongs to action. Therefore realm belongs to the historical dimension, royalty belongs to the ultimate dimension, and reign belongs to the dimension of action.

The ultimate dimension is the ground of being. The historical dimension is the kingdom of God or the phenomenal world, the world of birth and death. In the world of birth and death there is the presence of nirvana. And finally there is the dimension of action, the function of the kingdom, which is ruling the land that God the Father rules. How can people in that land live in such a way as to have peace, joy, and happiness? That is action. No matter what our tradition, when we are praying our priority is to arrive at the ultimate dimension, to arrive at the unborn and undying nature of life, to arrive at the kingdom of God; that is God.

When we practice walking meditation or enjoying a meal in mindfulness, we want nirvana to be there, we want nirvana to come to us in the present moment. Christians pray, sing psalms and hymns, receive the sacraments—all these are prayers directed to the aspiration *your kingdom come*, the aspiration that the kingdom of God be present in this very moment. If we're able to bring the ultimate dimension into the historical dimension, then we can live both dimensions at the same time. There is no reason why we can't touch the ultimate dimension while we are living in the historical dimension.

Your will be done on Earth as it is in heaven.

The unborn-undying nature of heaven, the happiness, solidity, and freedom of heaven do not only lie in the ultimate dimension, they also lie in the historical dimension. Thanks to the keys of the Three Dharma Seals, we're able to see that solidity, freedom, the unborn and the undying don't have to be looked for in nirvana, but can be found right in the world of birth and death; on this Earth as in heaven. In Vietnam a disciple asked a Zen master, "Where should I look for the unborn and the undying?" The master replied very clearly: "You should look for the unborn and undying right in the middle of birth and death." You should look for the water in the wave. It's very clear. Therefore we say: "your will be done on Earth as it is in heaven." This is the greatest aspiration that we have when we are praying.

Give us today our daily bread.

There is a French translation of this line that is very good: "Donnez-nous aujourd'hui notre pain de ce jour." *Notre pain de ce jour* is not the bread of every day, but of *this* day only. The word "aujourd'hui" (today) is already very good, but the words "de ce jour" (of this day) are even better. This sentence is a practice of trust. We do not have to demand our food for tomorrow, for the day after, and for the months and years to come. We only need to have food to eat today. I want to live deeply the present moment. This is similar to the Buddha's teaching in the Heart of the Prajñaparamita. "Form is emptiness," the Buddha says, but that in itself is not enough, so we have to add "...and emptiness is form," and then the teaching is complete.

In our daily life we have many anxieties. We have our cravings and we tend to want to store things up. We do not know that the present moment is important. Life can only be there in the present moment. If our only

concern is to invest in tomorrow, then it would be easy
to completely forget about the wonders of life in the
present moment. We have to return to the present
moment, to live it deeply and properly. We have to live
in such a way that the kingdom of God is present here
and now. This is a prayer that needs to be practiced
twenty-four hours every day, because we want to live
the present moment deeply in every second. The words
of the prayer are not only to be read before we go to
sleep; they have to be recited all day long.

We already have sufficient conditions to be happy
today. We have to pray in such a way that we can be in
touch with the conditions of happiness that are in us
and around us. They're all there, available. We shouldn't
be greedy. We shouldn't demand that life go on for
hundreds and hundreds of years. How can life continue for hundreds of years if right in this present
moment we are not able to be alive?

And forgive us our debts as we have also forgiven our debtors.

Our "debts" are the mistakes we've made towards our
loved ones. We've said something, we've done something, or we've thought something. Our words, our

actions, our thoughts have made the other person suffer, and these are the heavy debts we owe. How can we
live in such a way that every day we can forgive others?
We forgive because they do not have enough mindfulness, enough understanding, enough love, and they still
have wrong perceptions. So we have to be able to let go
of all of our resentment, because we also have made
mistakes of the same nature towards other people. If
we want our Father in heaven to forgive us, then we
also have to forgive others for their mistakes, the debts
that they have accumulated.

In our life, we may have made mistakes regarding our
parents, our brothers and sisters, our friends, and we
want to be forgiven. So we also have to forgive the short-
comings, the clumsiness, the faults, first above all of
those in our family, our blood family. This is a practice,
it is a prayer, a prayer we perform with our actions, and
with the way we live. We should remember that Jesus
himself taught the words of this prayer to his followers.

We may often have prayed well enough, but we still
have not learned the deepest art of prayer. If we have
a problem we call on the Buddha, we call on the bodhisattvas, we call on God to come and help us. There's

nothing wrong with that. We have the right to do it. But this kind of prayer is not made with the words of the greatest prayer, that is, to pray in such a way that we go beyond birth and death.

Often when we pray, it is because we want to ask God or the Buddha to do something that we cannot do. "Lord God, my loved one has a heart condition. God, please save him from this dangerous situation." We send messages like that to God. "Lord, my brother has cancer. Please heal my brother." In principle, God should know what he needs to do. But generally we just want to prescribe to God what he should do. We do this as if God does not know what is necessary, as if we need to say it clearly. But in fact, that one mind is much more wise than we are. What is even funnier, is that sometimes we bargain with the Buddha or with God. "Lord Buddha, if you give me that, then I will shave my head" or "I will be vegetarian for three months." Sometimes we are even more specific about the price: "If my son or daughter passes the exam, then I will make offerings to ten temples."

More than ten years ago I heard my close friend and disciple Sister Chan Khong praying in a similar way.

She said, "Lord Buddha, how would it be possible for Thây to live longer? If Thây can live a long time, then many people will benefit from the true teachings." (Thây is what my students and friends call me; it means "teacher" in Vietnamese.) Even in these words of prayer there is the idea of exchange. There are many people who will enjoy the profit of the true teachings and practice. Sister Chan Khong's heart was very great when she made that prayer. It seemed that she thought that the weak point of the Buddha was that he wanted his teachings to last for a long time and he wanted many people to be liberated by his teachings; therefore she used these scales: "Lord Buddha, if you allow my teacher to live for ten more years, then countless people will be able to profit from the teachings he gives." Isn't this a form of bargaining? This is a more subtle version of the prayer, "If my son or daughter passes the exam I will pray every day" or "If my friend gets better I will give up chocolate." It sounds as if when we give up chocolate, Buddha will benefit a great deal.

If we look a little bit deeper into the prayer of Sister Chan Khong, we will see something else, quite touching, beneath her words. She thinks that her teacher is her place of refuge and she is not yet solid enough, so that if her teacher was no longer to be with her then she would be lacking something. Therefore Sister Chan Khong also has the same state of mind as all her younger monastic sisters; she wants her teacher to live as long as possible. In that prayer there is a little bit of selfishness, the wish that we will not be left all alone, without a teacher. We want our place of refuge to be there for as long as possible. Is it not true that disciples want their teachers to live longer, as long as possible, so that many people can benefit from their teachings and so that all disciples will continue to have a place of refuge?

If your teacher passes away when you have only just been ordained as a monk or a nun, how sad that would be! So there is something likeable about the words of this prayer, and there is nothing wrong with it. But when we know how to look deeply as we pray, we shall be able to see what is happening in the depths of our consciousness. Praying like this could be very moving, but we have to look more deeply in order to see clearly, whether we are Buddhist or Christian or from another tradition: in our prayer do we have a general tendency to bargain with God, with the Buddha, even though we bargain in a very likeable way?

Do not lead us into temptation, but deliver us from evil.

"Temptation" means our trials of greed, anger, bitterness, suspicion, doubt, and lust. Some Christians would call them the temptations of Satan. In Buddhism, we call them the unwholesome actions of body, speech, and mind, and the temptations of the five senses: eyes, ears, nose, tongue, and body. Buddhism has another way of describing temptation: the three unwholesome destinies. There is the destiny of the hungry ghost realm. A hungry ghost is someone perpetually hungry for understanding and love, yet incapable of receiving it when it is offered. There is the destiny of the hell realms. In Buddhism, we are in the hell realms when we burn with anger, hatred, desire, envy, and other unwholesome states of mind. Temptation is also part of the third destiny, that of the animal realms. Of course, human beings are also animals. But here the animal realm means the world of those who simply follow their desires and whose hearts of love and understanding have never had a chance to be cultivated.

My experience has been that we are more easily

tempted into these realms when we are alone. When we are together with our community, with our brothers and sisters who are practicing, we are protected by the energy of the Sangha and it will not be easy for us to fall into temptation. So prayer can also be realized in action, not only in words. When we have mindfulness, when we have a Sangha, we find ourselves in a much more solid position and we don't have to fall into temptation.

When the Buddha was still in this world, people began the practice of reciting, "I take refuge in the Buddha." Taking refuge means to connect with that which is wholesome and supports us in our deepest aspiration. People did not wait for the Buddha to pass away to practice taking refuge in the Buddha. Also at that time, people began to recite, "I take refuge in the Sangha." Monks, nuns, and laypeople sat together and prayed. When monks, nuns, and laypeople sit together and pray, they are not only more able to resist temptation, but also to gather and strengthen their energy of mindfulness.

Today, many people live in the hell realms of drugs, loneliness, and despair. There are those who create hell for the people around them in many ways, and there are those who kill, steal, or rape. There are so many hungry ghosts wandering around, who are starved for love, understanding, a family, and an ideal.

We pray to avoid these three unwholesome paths. Our prayer can be very concrete once we have discovered a path to go on, once we have taken refuge in the Sangha, and once we know how to practice on a spiritual path. We pray to be guided away from the paths of temptation and encouraged on our spiritual path. This is an aspiration all of us can understand.

4

The Role of Prayer in Medicine

IN CHAPTER TWO, I wrote about three of the general aims of prayer: health, success, and love. I put health first because it is the foundation for everything that follows. But what is the relationship between health and prayer? Does renewed health come through prayer or through medicine or both?

Modern Medicine

Some medical scientists view illness as purely physiological. When there is sickness it is simply because something has gone wrong in the body. We think we only have to have a particular surgery or take the right number of pills and we will regain our health. This is still the prevailing view of illness.

In the last fifty years, Western medical science has made a great deal of progress in recognizing that the health of the body is connected to the health of the mind. We know that when our body suffers, our mind suffers as well. But the reverse may also be true. Sometimes we have a serious illness and nothing seems to be able to cure it. Perhaps we have frequent discomfort in our stomach. We have tried taking all kinds of medicine but it hasn't made any difference. This kind of discomfort could be connected to anxiety and grief. Our symptoms may arise from obstructions, worries, and suffering in our mind.

Of course, many illnesses begin in the body. Toxins in our environment, hereditary dispositions, age, and chance all play a part in creating illness. But even these illnesses have a mental component.

Medical science calls this connection of mind and body "psychosomatic." In Buddhism we also talk about "the oneness of body and mind." We call it *namarupa*, which means "name and form" in Sanskrit. Name and form is another way of saying body and mind. When medicine understands the oneness of body and mind, then medicine has accepted that nama (name) has an influence on rupa (form), and rupa has an influence on nama. If we have too much anxiety, then we could have stomach problems. If we have stomach problems, we can become depressed. So the body and the mind are always influencing each other.

The most helpful medical practitioner is one who knows how to look at the two aspects of a person, the physiological as well as the psychological, in order to suggest the best method of healing. Sitting meditation and mindful walking are particularly helpful with stress and depression-based illnesses. Studies with children have found that meditation can also affect what is called attention-deficit disorder in children. A University of Wisconsin study found that meditation not only reduced stress and anxiety, but also improved the functioning of the immune system.[7]

---

7 A summary of some of these findings can be found in this University of Wisconsin study at: http://www.sciencedaily.com /releases/2003/02/030204074125.htm, and on the Brooklyn College Website at: http://pc.brooklyn.cuny.edu/MED.htm.

Collective Medicine

There are also elements of healing that lie outside the body or mind of the individual.

These are the cultural and collective elements of health. When we are around those who are healthy and happy, we tend to be this way as well. When we are alone, we tend to get sick more often. But when we, as a culture, are stressed, angry, or engaged in warfare, then as a community we can also fall ill. When the collective consciousness is sick, we fall sick too.

For example, if we don't have an advanced degree, a good job, or a car, others think of us as not being capable, and we feel we are not normal, that we're not worth anything. The value of a person is based on having a degree, a good job, a car; this kind of thinking produces collective consciousness. When we do not have these things, we value ourselves less and feel we're not normal. But who among us is normal? And who has happiness? These are the real questions we have to ask. Countless people have a degree, a good job, and a car, but they still suffer, and often they even think that life is not worth living. But at the same time, there are people who don't have a degree, a good job, or a car, and are still happy and bring happiness to many others. If we keep allowing our mind and body to be influenced by negative beliefs, we will continually blame ourselves and feel that we are powerless and incapable. The sorrow and despair that result will make us sick.

Right now, the collective consciousness of our society is in very bad health. But we can learn to heal and transform ourselves. To do this we have to create a Sangha body, that is, a collective consciousness that is able to protect us. In the cities, you only need to look at the sights, listen to the sounds, and be in touch with a small number of people, and you can fall sick. When you come to a retreat space, you can close the door on all of that and open the door to the spiritual realm. Your body receives a physical, as well as a mental, boost.

A spiritual practice of prayer can remind us that happiness does not come from a degree, a job, or a car. We could call this kind of medicine that acknowledges the collective influence on our health "collective medicine" or "the medicine of the one mind." When something happens, even far away from us in time or space, it influences the one mind. Being able to see that is essential to understanding collective medicine.

Four hundred years ago the astronomer Johannes Kepler discovered that the moon influenced the Earth and caused the tides. When he shared his findings, nobody wanted to listen to him. The moon seemed so far away; how could it possibly influence the Earth? Even Galileo dismissed the idea.[8]

Our body is like the Earth. Not only those near us, but people, events, and actions thousands of miles away are capable of affecting it. What is happening now, what has happened in the past, what others are doing and thinking, all influence our health.

Many physicians see their job as solely to examine the body. A doctor may say, "Take off your clothes, breathe in, breathe out, open your mouth, stick out your tongue, say 'Ahhh,' here is the prescription, go get it filled, and take the medicine regularly." But, if we are

8 Johannes Kepler was a German astronomer and mathematician who lived from 1571 to 1630. Galileo Galilei was an Italian physicist, mathematician, and astronomer who lived from 1564 to 1642, and is credited with developing the telescope in 1609 in order to be able to look at the universe.

ill, we may also need spiritual healing. We need someone to say, "We are sitting here, let us breathe together.
Let us calm our mind so that it can be still."

Doctors, nurses, and other health practitioners
could practice sitting meditation and conscious breathing before they come to work. Once they have finished
examining patients for the day, and have given out prescriptions and gone home, doctors could sit and meditate on the health of their patients. Families and
friends of people who are ill could do the same. Instead
of simply saying, "My sister is sick, so I'm going to
take her to the doctor; that's all I can do," we could
also just sit with our sister, breathing in and out.

In this collective consciousness of health, we take
responsibility for the health of our loved ones. We live
mindfully, as free people without too many preoccupa-
tions. In our hearts, we have the energy of love and
prayer.

Dr. Larry Dossey says we have to open the door for
this third collective stage of medical science. He
believes that doctors who discourage people from praying are doing their patients a real disservice. When we
pray, we calm our mind, we feel peace and joy, and in

that way we create a source of energy that can be helpful to a person in ill health.

When we are in a community, a Sangha, we know
that the mindfulness, peace, joy, and freedom of each
member of the Sangha is very much linked to our own
health and that of our loved ones. In meditation, we
can direct their loving kindness and compassion to our
loved ones. When we are able to produce the energy of
loving kindness and compassion in our heart, that
energy will heal our own body and mind. Only then
can our energy heal the body and mind of our loved
ones.

The energy lies in the collective consciousness, so it
does not need to travel from one point to another in
space. I have mentioned my student, Thay Dam
Nguyen, who was ill. Although I am in France and she
is in Vietnam, the moment I practice sitting meditation and send her the energy of loving kindness she
receives it. During meditation time I have been sending
loving kindness and compassion to others as well, and
I am sure that there will be a result, whether it is small
or great. Maybe it will be less of a result than we would
want, but there will be a result.

When my friends pray for me, I am sure that I receive the energy. And when I pray for them, they are certain to receive more energy. Since we know and love each other, it is very easy for us to produce the energy of compassion and love in our heart for each other. What Larry Dossey calls the Absolute, or God, is the one mind. In that one mind there are great amounts of energy. If we use the energy of loving kindness and compassion meditation to be in touch with the energy of the one mind, we can transform and change our situation.

The Buddha has a teaching called the Twelve Nidanas. Each *nidana* is a link of conditioned arising. In conditioned arising, each link represents one of the physical or psychological phenomena that make up an individual, and each link causes the arising of the next. The twelve links are depicted as a circle. Within the twelve nidanas, the *ayatanas*, the six sense organs (eyes, ears, nose, tongue, body, and mind) arise based on mind and form. When the six sense organs are in touch with the six sense objects, then mind and form may be disturbed and can become sick. We need to train in our practice so that the six sense organs don't become a source of ill health. We can guard the six sense organs with our awareness, to protect ourselves from the many unwholesome influences, both physical and psychological, that are around us. With mindfulness, we are aware of what is entering us, just as a guard at the city gate knows who is coming in and going out.

Our practice in Plum Village is that when the six sense organs are in touch with the six sense objects, we use our diligence and awareness to guard ourselves. We have to stand guard at the doors of the six ayatanas so that we don't fall sick.

It is not enough to study medical science for six years at university. University medical schools don't teach us how to diagnose illness by looking into the store consciousness.

Store consciousness, also called *alaya* consciousness, is the deepest part of our psyche. It contains all the seeds of the happiness, sadness, jealousy, and other emotions we experience. These seeds, when watered or touched, appear as zones of energy. Store consciousness is like a garden that contains all kinds of seeds, and mind consciousness is like the gardener. When we are practicing meditation, mind consciousness is working; but store consciousness is also working secretly day and night. The unconscious mind of Western psychology is only one part of store consciousness. If we can recognize and transform the internal knots that lie deeply in our consciousness, it will bring us to liberation and healing. That is called transformation at the base (*asrayaparavritti*). It means the transformation that takes place right in the substructure of consciousness.

Although psychiatrists are taught about diagnosing sickness in the unconscious, what they speak of as the unconscious is only a small part of our store consciousness. When we live in an unhealthy environment, the negative thinking, speaking, and actions of that environment influence us, and sooner or later we may fall sick. Living in an environment where people seek only to satisfy sensual desires can cause collective suffering, despair, and depression. We destroy our bodies and minds and close the door to the future. If we want to have good health, we have to be determined to develop a good environment. We have to find a wholesome environment and practice living a wholesome life. A larger community that is committed to spiritual, physical, and mental health is our best opportunity for healing.

Any doctor who practices the medicine of the one mind should know how to guide his patients on the path of healing. Alaya consciousness is a collective consciousness. It gives rise to rivers, mountains, lakes, ponds, air, water, birds, and fish. Whether the environmental retribution is beautiful or ugly depends on whether we have been treading an unwholesome path or a wholesome path that goes in the direction of a healthy environment.

If our loved ones, our doctor, and our community know how to produce the energy of love and of prayer to send in our direction and embrace us, then we can help our bodies recover their health. Sometimes we are in such ill health that nothing seems to help, neither the medicines we buy nor the exercise we do. The collective consciousness can't necessarily cure us, but if we can be in touch with a wholesome collective consciousness, our healing is more effective.

Praying and sending spiritual energy to those who are sick, as we do in Buddhism, is very important for their healing. In Buddhism, we have much faith in the energy of this kind of prayer, but we call it "sending spiritual energy." Our faith is not superstition, because we know that this kind of prayer, this sending of spiritual energy, is based on truths that are very scientific. The truth is that when the community sits together and produces the energy of mindful recollection, or awareness, in order to send spiritual support, then quite surely that energy will reach our loved one. We also know that consciousness can be created and nourished by ignorance. The more ignorance there is, the more we will have further causes of ill health. Our daily practice, and that of our friends and our society, can create clarity. When clarity and understanding are produced, there is love and compassion. When there is more understanding, there is more love in the collective consciousness, and the state of health improves, not only of the individual but also of the community as a whole.

5

Meditation and Healing

MEDITATION (called *dhyana* in Sanskrit and *zen* in Japanese) is the marrow of Buddhist practice. The aim of meditation is to help the practitioner arrive at a deep understanding of reality. This insight has the capacity to liberate us from fear, anxiety, and melancholy. It can produce understanding and compassion, raise the quality of life, and bring freedom, peace, and joy to ourselves and to others around us.

Especially in the last part of the twentieth century, people in the West have begun to give their attention to meditation. The material comforts of the West are not enough to make happiness. Our grief, our concerns, and our problems can only be resolved by living a spiritual life. Buddhism and the practice of meditation are presently giving a large number of people a way to respond to these difficulties.

Sitting meditation is the most common kind of meditation, but we can also practice meditation in other positions, such as walking, standing, and lying down. When we wash clothes, chop wood, water the vegetables, or drive the car—wherever we are, whatever we are doing, in whatever position our body happens to be, if the energies of mindfulness, concentration, and insight are present in our mind and body, then we are practicing meditation. We do not have to go to a temple, a church, or a meditation center to practice meditation. Living in society, going to work every day, looking after our family, are also opportunities for us to practice meditation. Meditation has the effect of nourishing and healing body and mind. And it brings the joy of living back to the practitioner and to those in her life.

Meditation's Three Sources of Energy

Meditation produces three sources of energy: mindfulness, concentration, and insight. Mindfulness is a source of energy that helps us to be aware of what is happening in the present moment—in our body, in our mind, and in our environment. The full term is Right Mindfulness (*samyak smṛti*). What is happening in the present moment in the field of our body, our mind, and our environment is diverse and vast. We cannot possibly recognize all of it in one moment. But we are able to recognize what stands out in relief and that which we need to recognize most of all. When we give our attention to our breathing, and we recognize an in-breath as an in-breath or an out-breath as an out-breath, this is called the practice of mindfulness of breathing. If we give our attention to our steps and can recognize each step that we place on the floor of our house or on the earth, this is called mindfulness of making steps.

If we are angry and we are aware that we are angry, that is called mindfulness of anger. When we are practicing mindfulness of anger, there are two kinds of energy manifesting in us. The first energy is that of anger. The second energy is that of right mindfulness, produced by our mindful meditation. The second energy recognizes and embraces the first energy. If we can practice for five or seven minutes, then the energy of right mindfulness will penetrate the energy of anger and some of the energy of anger will be transformed.

The energy of mindfulness carries with it the energy of concentration. Concentration gives rise to the energy of insight, and insight is able to transform anger into understanding, acceptance, compassion, and reconciliation. In our daily life, our mind has the tendency to think about the past or worry about the future. Our body is present, but our mind is not present. Right mindfulness is the energy that helps us bring our mind back to our body, so that we can be authentically present here and now. If we are present in that way, we can be in touch with what is wonderful in life inside us and around us.

In the spirit of meditation, life is only really present in the here and the now. The Buddha taught, "The past is already gone. The future has not yet come. Life can only be touched in the present moment."[9] When we can be in touch with what is wonderful in the present moment, we are nourished and healed. When our

9 Bhaddekaratta Sutta, Majjhima Nikaya 131.

energy of right mindfulness has become solid, we can use it to recognize and embrace our suffering and pain, our anger and hatred, our greed, violence, jealousy, and despair. Then we can transform these things bit by bit. Dwelling peacefully in the present moment can bring about wonderful healing, and we can take ourselves out of the clutches of regret about and attachment to the past, and of our worries and fear about the future.

The Four Fields of Mindfulness

Mindfulness is always mindfulness of something; mindfulness always has to have an object. The four categories of objects of mindfulness are: our body, our feelings, our mind, and the objects of our mind. These four fields are called the Four Establishments of Mindfulness. When the energy of mindfulness recognizes the body, it helps us return and care for the body, allowing our body to relax. In Buddhism this is called "pacifying the body formation." This is a very effective practice for dealing with the stress in our body and nervous system. We can practice this when we are lying down or sitting. This practice helps our body to heal itself in a natural way. If we are healing ourselves with prescriptions or medicine, then this method of relaxing our body can help us recover much more quickly.

Practicing mindfulness of the body keeps us from consuming toxins. It helps us to walk, stand, work, and behave in a free way, and raises the quality of our daily life. The practice of mindfulness of our feelings helps us recognize our feeling in the moment, whether it is a pleasant, unpleasant, or neutral feeling. By "recognize," I mean we are able to come to the source of those mental formations and to know clearly their essence and transform them. For example, if with the energy of mindfulness we are able to recognize the symptoms of depression, we have the opportunity to look deeply into the nature and root of the depression in order to know the near and distant causes that have brought it about. Using mindfulness to look after the depression and to bring our mind into contact with refreshing phenomena that have the capacity to nourish and heal, we can alleviate the depression. And with mindfulness we can keep ourselves from consuming or being in touch with items, images, sounds, and thoughts which bring us into a state of tension, anxiety, and melancholy. In this way, we do not allow our depression to continue and be nourished by these poisons.

According to Buddhist psychology, we have fifty-one kinds of mental phenomena, called mental formations, that include positive states of mind, like love and inclusiveness; negative states of mind, like anger and despair; and undetermined states of mind, such as thoughtfulness and regret. Whatever the mental formation, mindfulness helps us understand why and from where it has arisen and what lasting effect it will have on our body and mind. With concentration and insight, we will be able to notice and be pleased by pleasant emotions and transform negative and unpleasant emotions. If the feeling is neutral, then with mindfulness it can become a pleasant feeling. For example, when we have a toothache, we have an unpleasant feeling. We think that if our toothache went away, we would have a pleasant feeling. But generally when we don't have toothache, we just have a neutral feeling; we do not feel happy because we do not have a toothache. When we are aware of the non-toothache, it will help us change the neutral feeling into a feeling of well-being.

More and more places in the West use the practice

of mindfulness to heal physical pain, depression, and relieve stress in the body and mind. At the University of Massachusetts Medical School, for example, Professor Jon Kabat-Zinn conducts a program of healing based on mindfulness meditation called the Stress Reduction Clinic. Through this program, practitioners are able to heal physical pain, stress, and disease quite effectively. At large university medical schools such as Harvard and the University of California at Los Angeles, there are departments doing research on the role of meditation in helping heal mental and physical illness.

The Mind/Body Medical Institute at Harvard University was created and directed by Professor Herbert Benson. This institute is doing research, teaching meditation, and applying it in healing. The institute has worked without interruption for the past thirty-five years. According to Professor Benson, many scientists, doctors, psychologists, educators, and nurses have been trained to a high level at the institute, and then have gone on to guide research programs and make discoveries in various fields. They have seen that meditation can bring about a great deal of healing. A number of medical programs have been developed that offer effective ways of reducing symptoms and healing illness by relieving tension in the mind.

In the past thirty years, the laboratories of the medical faculty at Harvard have, in a systematic way, researched the benefits brought about by the influence of body and mind on each other. The research programs have proven that when people repeat a phrase from a sacred scripture or the words of a guided meditation, or even a single sacred sound, it stops the dispersed state of the mind from intervening, and positive physical changes can take place, changes contrary to those that brought about the mental tension to begin with. The research programs have demonstrated the beneficial nature of the changes brought about by meditation practice and have shown that they can have an effect on such medical conditions as high blood pressure, irregular heartbeat, chronic pain, insomnia, and impotence.

The fourth and final field of mindfulness is mindfulness of the objects of our perception, such as mountains, rivers, trees, plants, people, things, society. When the energy of mindfulness, concentration, and insight is powerful, we are able to arrive at a deep insight into reality, and we are able to realize great freedom. We are no longer attached to our feelings of worry, craving, hatred, and despair. Buddha and the holy ones achieved this insight and have the great freedom called liberation. When we practice meditation, we also arrive at freedom, and although our freedom may not yet be great, we still can undo many wrong perceptions and prejudices, and we do not suffer nearly as much as we did before. In fact, we have a great deal of peace and joy in our life in the present moment.

Tangled Knots

Meditation is particularly able to help us with what Buddhism calls internal knots and identity complexes. These fetters keep us from being able to be in the present moment.

Internal knots are collections of delusion, repression, fear, and anxiety that have been tied in the depths of our consciousness. They have the capacity to bind us and to direct us to do, say, and think things that in reality we don't want to do, say, or think. Internal knots are sown and nourished by our lack of mindfulness in daily life. The ten chief internal knots are: greed; hatred; ignorance; conceit; suspicion; attachment to the body as the self; extreme views and prejudices; clinging to rites and rituals; our craving for immortality; and our craving to keep everything just as it is. Our health and our happiness depend to a great extent on our ability to transform these ten fetters.

Mindfulness has the capacity to recognize internal knots when they appear in our consciousness. These internal knots have been formed in the past, sometimes as habit energies transmitted to us by our parents and grandparents. We do not need to go back into the past and dig into memories, as they do in psychology, in order to discover the roots of these troubled, tangled parts of our mind. The energy of mindfulness has the capacity to recognize internal formations when they manifest themselves and to look deeply into them so we are able to see the roots of these tangled knots.

Meditation practice helps us to see the interconnection and interdependence of everything that is. There is no phenomenon, human or otherwise, that can arise on its own and endure independently. This relies on that; one thing relies on another in order to arise and

endure. This is the insight of interdependence, sometimes called interbeing or nonself. Nonself means there
isn't a separate permanent entity. All things are in a
constant state of change. Father and son, for example,
are not entirely separate realities. Father exists in son,
and son exists in father. Son is the continuation of
father into the future, and father is the continuation
of son back to the source. The happiness of the son is
linked to the happiness of the father. If the father is
not happy, then the happiness of the son cannot be
perfect. The nature of all things is non-self. There is no
separate and independent self.

In the world of psychotherapy, low self-esteem is
spoken of as a sickness. In mindfulness practice, both
low and high self-esteem as well as needing to think
yourself exactly equal to someone else, are also con-
sidered sicknesses or, as we say in Buddhism, complexes. All three of these complexes are founded on the
idea of a separate self. They are all based on pride:
pride of being better, pride of being worse, pride of
being equal. Suffering, which arises from anger, jealousy, hatred, and shame can only be completely transformed when we come to the insight of no-self. This

is the basis of the practice of healing in meditation.

Zen Master Thuong Chieu of eleventh-century Vietnam taught that if we understand the activities of the mind, then meditation practice will become easy. The Consciousness Only school of Buddhism talks about eight kinds of consciousnesses: the five sense consciousnesses (eye, ear, nose, tongue, and body); mind consciousness; *manas* (the energy which is attached to the idea that there is a separate self, independent and everlasting, and opposed to those things that are not self); and store consciousness.

When our deep desires, fears, and feelings of indignation are repressed in our store consciousness, they are like seeds that cannot get the oxygen and water they need to grow and transform into something beautiful, and we can experience symptoms in both the body and the mind that result from this blockage. Although these mental formations have been repressed, they can still bind us and direct us, and so they become very strong internal knots. We have the habit of ignoring them in the hope that they won't have the opportunity to come up and appear in our mind consciousness. We seek forgetfulness in consumption. We don't want to face these feelings of pain and despondency. We want to fill the area of mind consciousness so that all the space is occupied and the feelings of pain that lie in the basement have no place to come up to. So we watch television, we listen to the radio, we look at books, read newspapers, have conversations, gamble, and drink alcohol in order to forget.

When our blood is unable to circulate well, symptoms of sickness arise in our body. In the same way, when the mental formations are repressed and cannot circulate, then symptoms of mental and physical illness begin to appear. We need to know how to stop repressing, so that the mental formations of desire, fear, indignation and so on have an opportunity to arise, be recognized, and be transformed. Cultivating the energy of mindfulness through meditation can help us do this. Producing mindfulness through the daily practice of meditation will help us recognize, embrace, and transform our feelings of suffering.

When we recognize and embrace these mental formations instead of forcing them back underground, their negative energy lessens a little. Just meditating on these mental formations for five or ten minutes can help. The next time they arise, they will be recognized and embraced again and will return to the store consciousness a little bit weaker. Practicing like this, we no longer fear our negative mental formations; we no longer push them down or repress them as we did before. The good circulation in our mind can be reestablished, and the psychological complications that cause blocks in the body can slowly disappear.

True Happiness

Mindfulness is above all the capacity simply to recognize the presence of an object without taking sides, without judging, and without craving or despising that object. For example, suppose we have a zone of pain in our body. With mindfulness, we simply recognize that pain. This is a very different kind of prayer than you may be used to, but sitting in meditation and simply being aware of that pain is still prayer. With the energy of concentration and insight, we may be able to see and understand its importance and the real reason for its arising. We may be able to cure it based on the understanding that comes from mindfulness and concentration. If we have too much anxiety, if we are always imagining things, then this anxiety and these imaginings will bring stress into our mind and the pain will increase. It isn't cancer but we imagine that it is cancer and we can worry and grieve until we are not able to eat or sleep. The pain doubles and can lead to a more serious condition.

In the Puttamansa Sutra, the Buddha gives the example of two arrows. If a second arrow is planted in the wound caused by the first arrow, then the pain will be not only double but increase tenfold. We should not allow a second arrow or a third arrow to come and do even more harm to us because of our imaginings and our worries.

When we pursue the objects of sensual desire, such as money, fame, power, and sex, we are not able to produce true happiness. Rather, we create a great deal of suffering for ourselves and for others. Human beings are full of desires. Day and night, they run after these desires, and therefore they are not free. If they are not free, they do not feel at ease and they do not feel happy. If we have few desires, we are satisfied with a simple, wholesome life and we have the time to live deeply

every moment of daily life and to love and look after
our dear ones. That is the secret of true happiness. In
our present society, far too many people are looking
for happiness by satisfying their sensual desires. The
quantity of suffering and despair has greatly increased.

The Sutra in the Forest talks about desire as a trap.
If we are caught in the trap of desire, we will grieve and
lose all our freedom, and we cannot have true happiness. Fear and anxiety also create suffering. If we have
enough understanding to accept living a simple life and
being content with what we have, we will not need to
worry and fear anymore. It is only because we think
that tomorrow we could lose our profession and not
receive our monthly salary that we constantly live in a
state of nervousness and anxiety. So, the way of consuming little and making much happiness is the only
way out for our present-day civilization.

This book began with the question of why we pray.
Perhaps, really, all energy of prayer comes back to our
simple human desire for happiness and being connected
both to other people and to something greater than ourselves. Prayer, whether silent, chanted, or in meditation,
is a way to return to ourselves in the present moment

and touch the peace that is there. It is, simultaneously, a way to put us in touch with the universal and the timeless. Our true happiness comes from being fully conscious in the present moment, aware of our connection to everything else in the universe.

Meditation Exercises

FOLLOWING are five simple meditation exercises that carry within them the essence of practical meditation. The first four exercises have the capacity to nourish. The fifth exercise has the capacity to heal.[10]

Each exercise begins with words that can be said to yourself while you are sitting in meditation. At first, you may want to say the whole sentence. Then, you might just say the shorter phrase written to the right of the sentence. For example, with your inhale, you say "calm" to yourself. With your exhale, you say the word "smile."

10 These exercises are adapted from *Blooming of a Lotus* by Thich Nhat Hanh (Boston, MA: Beacon Press, 1993).

Exercise One:
Calming the Mental Formations

Breathing in, I feel calm.   Calm
Breathing out, I smile.   Smile

Breathing in, I dwell   Present moment
in the present moment.
Breathing out, it is the   Wonderful
most wonderful moment.   moment

Many people begin their practice of meditation with this exercise. Others, though they have practiced this exercise for a long time, still practice it because it continues to bring them much benefit. Breathing in, we give our attention to our breath. We feel the calmness for as long as we are breathing in. Just as when we drink a cool glass of water, our insides feel cool. In meditation practice, whenever the mind is calm and peaceful the body is also calm and peaceful, because the conscious breath brings the body and the mind together again. When breathing out we smile in order to relax all the muscles in our face; there are about three hundred of them. Our nervous system is also relaxed when we smile. The smile is the result of feeling calm from our breathing in, and the smile is also a cause that helps us to become relaxed and feel the peace and joy that is clearly increasing in us.

The second breath brings us back to the present moment and puts an end to all the attachments we have to the past and all the anxieties we have about the future, so we are able to dwell peacefully here and now. Life is only present in the here and the now. Therefore we have to return to the present moment in order to be in touch with life. This breath helps us to realize the joy of being alive and puts us in touch with the reality of life. If we know that we are living, and we know that we can be in touch with all the wonderful things of life in us and around us, that is a miracle. We only need to open our eyes to look, or our ears to listen, and we can receive the wonderful things of life. Therefore the present moment can be the most beautiful and wonderful moment if we practice living in an awakened way with the help of our breathing. We can also practice the first part of the exercise many times before we go on to the second part. This exercise can be practiced anywhere: in the meditation hall, on the train, in the kitchen, by the bank of a river, in the park, whether we are walking, standing, lying, or sitting down, or even working.

Exercise Two:
Calming and Relaxing the Bodily Formation

Breathing in, I know I'm breathing in.   In
Breathing out, I know I'm breathing out.   Out

Breathing in, my breath grows deep.   Deep
Breathing out, my breath grows slow.   Slow

Breathing in, I am aware   Aware
of my whole body.   of body
Breathing out, I relax my   Relaxing
whole body.   body

Breathing in, I calm my whole body.   Calm body
Breathing out, I love my body.   Love body

Breathing in, I smile to my whole body.	Smile
Breathing out, I ease my whole body.	Ease
Breathing in, I smile to my whole body.	Smile
Breathing out, I release the tension in my body.	Release
Breathing in, I feel joyful.	Joy
Breathing out, I taste the source of peace and joy.	Peace
Breathing in, I dwell in the present moment.	Present moment
Breathing out, it is a wonderful moment.	Wonderful moment
Breathing in, my sitting posture is solid.	Solid
Breathing out, I feel stable.	Stable

This exercise, though it is easy to practice, has a very great effect. People who have only just begun to practice meditation can, thanks to this exercise, immediately feel the peace and joy of meditation practice. On the other hand, people who have been practicing meditation for a long time can still practice this exercise in order to continue to bring peace and nourishment to both the body and the mind, so that they will be able to go further on the path of healing by means of meditation.

The first two lines (in, out) help you recognize the breath; if it is the in-breath, then you know that it is the in-breath; if it is the out-breath, you know it is the out-breath. If we practice like this a couple of times, then automatically we will stop thinking about the past, about the future, and we'll also put an end to other unnecessary thinking. The reason is that the mind of the practitioner has entirely gone into the breath in order to recognize the breath. Thanks to that, the mind becomes one with the breath. Now the mind is no longer a mind of anxiety or of thinking about the past, but is just the mind of breathing.

In the second breath (deep, slow), we are able to see

that the in-breath is deeper and the out-breath is slower. This happens quite naturally. It does not need the express effort of the practitioner. Breathing in with the awareness that we are breathing in, just as in the first exercise, the breath naturally becomes deeper, slower, more harmonious, and so has a higher quality. When the breath has become more harmonious, peaceful, and rhythmic, then you begin to have a feeling of peace and joy in body and mind. Peacefulness of the breath brings with it the peacefulness of body and mind. Now you have begun to enjoy Dharma happiness, the joy of meditation.

In the third breath (awareness of the whole body, relaxing the whole body), the in-breath brings the mind back to the body and helps the mind to become acquainted with the body again. The breath is the bridge that crosses from the body to the mind and from the mind to the body. The out-breath has the effect of relaxing the whole body. While breathing out, make all the muscles relax in the shoulders, the arms, in the whole body, so that the feeling of relaxation can enter the whole body. This breathing should be practiced at the very least ten times.

In the fourth breath (calming the whole body, sending love to the whole body), the in-breath helps you make the body calm and peaceful. With the out-breath, you express compassion and care for the whole body. The fourth part of the exercise makes the whole body calm, and helps you practice showing compassion in order to be in touch with your own body.

The fifth breath (smiling to the whole body, easing the whole body) allows us to release the tension in all the muscles of our face. You send that smile to your whole body like a cool stream of water. Easing means making the body feel light and at ease. This breathing is also aimed at nourishing the whole body with the compassion the practitioner has for his body.

The sixth breath (smiling to the whole body, releasing the tension in the whole body) continues the fifth breath. This breath dissolves all the tensions still there in the body.

In the seventh breath (feeling joyful, tasting peace) you receive the feeling of joy resulting from being able to see that you are still alive, still in good health, and have an opportunity to look after and nourish your spirit as well as your body. The out-breath is accompanied by a feeling of happiness. Happiness is always something simple. Sitting still and breathing with awareness can already be happiness. So many people are whirling around like a propeller, their lives so busy every day, without the opportunity to taste this Dharma happiness.

The eighth breath (dwelling in the present moment, it is a wonderful moment) brings you back to dwell in the present moment. Buddha taught that the past is already gone, the future has not yet come, and life is only available in the present moment. To return to the present moment and abide there is truly to return to life. Right in the present moment, you are able to be in touch with everything that is wonderful in life: peace, joy, liberation, Buddha nature, nirvana, all can be discovered only in the present moment. Happiness lies only in the present moment. Our breathing helps us to be in touch with these wonderful things and brings about a great deal of happiness for ourselves. We are able to truly feel that the present moment is a wonderful moment.

The ninth breath (my posture is solid, I enjoy the stability) brings your attention to your body's posture.

If the posture is not yet straight and beautiful, it will now become straight and beautiful. The solid sitting posture brings about the feeling of stability in body and in mind. Right in the moment that we are sitting in this way, we feel that we are the sovereign of our body and mind. We are not being carried away by the actions of body, speech, or mind that can overwhelm us.

Exercise Three:
Nourishing the Body

Breathing in, I know I'm breathing in.	In
Breathing out, I know I'm breathing out.	Out
Breathing in, my breath grows deep.	Deep
Breathing out, my breath grows slow.	Slow
Breathing in, I calm my body.	Calm
Breathing out, I feel at ease.	Ease
Breathing in, I smile.	Smile
Breathing out, I release.	Release

| Breathing in, dwelling in the present moment. | Present moment |
| Breathing out, it is a wonderful moment. | Wonderful moment |

This exercise can be practiced anywhere: in the meditation hall, in the living room, in the kitchen, or on the train.

The first breath is to bring the body and mind back together to be one. At the same time it helps us return to dwell in the present moment and be in touch with the wonderful life which is happening in this present moment. After we have breathed like this for two or three minutes, our breath quite naturally becomes lighter, freer, more gentle, slower, deeper, and then we feel really at ease in our body and in our mind.

In the second breath (deep, slow), we can dwell with this breath for as long as we like. Then we go on to the third breath (calm, ease). Here we are aware of the ease and the calmness of our body and mind, and the joy of meditation continues to nourish us. In the Zen school, there is the sentence: "The joy of meditation is our daily food." It means that the joy we have when we practice meditation is used as a food to nourish the practitioner. The fourth breath (smile, release) and the fifth breath (present moment, wonderful moment) we have already practiced in the first exercise.

Exercise Four:
Finding Nourishment in Nature

Breathing in, I know I'm breathing in.	In
Breathing out, I know I'm breathing out.	Out
Breathing in, I see myself as a flower.	Flower
Breathing out, I feel fresh.	Fresh
Breathing in, I see myself as a mountain.	Mountain
Breathing out, I feel solid.	Solid
Breathing in, I become calm water.	Water
Breathing out, I reflect the sky and the mountains.	Reflecting

Breathing in, I become the vastness of space.	Space
Breathing out, I feel infinite freedom.	Free

This exercise can be practiced at the beginning of all sessions of meditation. Or it can be practiced for the whole of the sitting meditation session to nourish body and mind, to quiet body and mind, and to arrive at letting go and freedom.

The first breath can be practiced many times until we arrive at the state of oneness of body and mind. We bring our body and mind together so they are one.

The second breath brings us freshness. A human being should be fresh as a flower because we are flowers in the garden of the universe. We only need to look at the beautiful children in order to see that. Their two round eyes are flowers. Their bright face and gentle forehead is a flower. Their two hands are flowers. It's only because we worry so much that our forehead has wrinkles, only because we cry so much and go through so many sleepless nights that dark circles form under our eyes. Breathing in, we revive our own flower nature. Breathing in brings our flower back to life. Breathing out helps us be aware that we can be as fresh, that we are as fresh as a flower. This is a loving kindness meditation for us.

The third breath, seeing that we are a solid mountain, will help us to stand solidly in the moments when we are deeply moved by strong emotions. When we fall into a state of despair, anxiety, fear, or anger, we can feel that we are going through a storm. But we can be like the trunk of a tree standing firmly in the storm. If we look at a tree that is standing in a storm, we see that the branches at the top of the tree are swaying back and forth as if they could be broken off or blown down by the wind at any moment. But if we look down at the trunk of the tree, especially towards the roots, we see that the roots of the tree are holding firmly to the earth; we see that the tree is more solid down there and we feel more at peace. Our body and our mind are the same. In the storm of our emotions, if we know how to remove ourselves from the hurricane area, the area of our brain, and bring all our attention down to our abdomen, to the acupressure point just below the navel, we will feel very different. We will see that we are not only our emotions, we are more than our emotions. The emotions come and then they go, but we remain. When we are overwhelmed by our emotions, we feel so frail and fragile, and we think that we can lose our life.

There are people who do not know how to deal with their strong emotions. When they are suffering too much because of their despair, fear, or anger, they think that the only way to put an end to their suffering is to put an end to their own life. So many people, many of them young, have killed themselves. If we know how to sit down in the lotus position and practice breathing, then we can overcome these difficult moments.

We can also practice this breathing in the lying down position of total relaxation. We can breathe in accord with the rising and falling of our abdomen and give our attention wholly to our abdomen. In this way we are out of the danger zone and we are not carried away by the storm. We should practice like this until our spirit is calm and the storm has passed and we know that the danger is over. But we should not wait until our mind is suffering in order to practice. If we do not have the habit of practicing, we will forget to practice when we need to, and we will allow our emotions to overwhelm us and carry us away. We should practice every day in order to have a good habit, and in that way when the strong emotions come along, we shall know how to practice to deal with them and master them. We should also show young people how to practice healing meditation to help them overcome their too-strong emotions.

The aim of the fourth breath (water, reflecting) is to calm our body and mind. In the Sutra on the Full Awareness of Breathing, the Buddha taught: Breathing in, I calm my mind. When our mind is not calm, our perceptions are usually wrong. What we see, hear, and think does not reflect reality, just as when there are waves on the lake, its waters cannot faithfully reflect the clouds in the sky. Buddha is the cool full moon passing through the sky of emptiness. If the mind of living beings is calm, then the moon's image will be reflected clearly. Our sadness and anger arise from our wrong perceptions. So in order to avoid wrong perceptions, we have to train ourselves so that our mind is peaceful as the surface of the lake on an autumn morning. Our breath is to bring about this peace.

Space, free is the fifth breath. If we have too many occupations and concerns, we will not have any leisure, peace, or joy. This breath is aimed at bringing space back to us—space in our heart and space around us. If we have many anxieties, calculations, and plans, then we should reduce them. Our sadness and anger are like that. We have to practice to let them go. These different kinds of baggage just make our life heavier. Often we think that if we did not have all this baggage—our office, our position, our reputation, our work, our importance—that we would not be happy. But if we look again, we see that nearly all this baggage is just an obstacle to our happiness. When we can let go of it, we will be happy.

The Buddha's happiness was very great. One day, while sitting in the Great Forest outside of Vaishali, the Buddha saw a farmer passing by. The farmer asked the Buddha if he had seen his cows which had run away. And besides that, he said, maggots had eaten the two acres of sesame he had planted last year. He said that he was the unhappiest person alive, and maybe he should kill himself. The Buddha told him he had not seen his cows so he might find them in another direction. After he had gone, Buddha turned around and smiled to the bhikshus who were sitting with him, and said, "Monks, do you know that you are happy and free? You do not have a single cow to lose." If we practice this breathing it helps us let go of our cows—the cows in our mind and the cows outside ourselves.

Exercise Five:
Healing

Breathing in, I see myself as a five-year-old child.	Five-year-old child
Breathing out, I smile to the five-year-old child.	I smile
Breathing in, I see the five-year-old child, who is myself, as very fragile and vulnerable.	Five-year-old child fragile and vulnerable
Breathing out, I smile to the five-year-old child in myself, with understanding and compassion.	Smiling with understanding and compassion

Breathing in, I see my father
as a five-year-old child.

Father
five years old

Breathing out, I smile to my
father as a five-year-old child.

I smile

Breathing in, I see that
five-year-old child who is
my father as very fragile
and vulnerable.

Five-year-old
father
vulnerable
and fragile

Breathing out, I smile to
the five-year-old child who is
my father with understanding
and compassion.

Smiling with
understanding
and compassion

Breathing in, I see my mother
as a five-year-old child.

Mother
five years old

Breathing out, I smile to my
mother as a five-year-old child.

I smile

Breathing in, I see my mother
as a five-year-old child,
fragile and vulnerable.

Breathing out, I smile
with compassion.

My five-year-old
mother, vulner-
rable and fragile

Smiling with
understanding
and compassion

Breathing in, I see the suffering
of my father when he was
five years old.

Breathing out, I see the suffering
of my mother when she was
five years old.

Father suffering
at five years old

Mother suffer-
ing at five years
old

Breathing in, I see my father
in myself.

Breathing out, I smile
to my father in myself.

My father
in myself

I smile

Breathing in, I see my mother
in myself.

My mother
in myself

Breathing out, I smile
to my mother in myself.

I smile

Breathing in, I understand
the difficulties of my
father in me.

Difficulties of
my father
in me

Breathing out, I vow to
transform my father and
myself together.

Transforming
father and
self together

Breathing in, I understand
the difficulties of my
mother in me.

Difficulties of
my mother
in me

Breathing out, I vow to
transform the difficulties of
my mother and myself together.

Transforming
mother and
self together

This exercise has helped many young people to be able to reestablish a good relationship between themselves and their parents and to transform their internal formations that were formed when they were young children. There are people who cannot think about their father or mother without feeling hatred and grief. The seed of love is always there in the mother or father's heart and in the son or the daughter also. But because we do not know how to water that seed, and especially because we do not know how to resolve the internal formations which have been sown and have ceaselessly developed in our mind, both generations find it very difficult to accept each other.

In the first step, visualize yourself as a five-year-old child. At that age, we are very easily wounded; a stern look or a harsh or critical word can bring about wounds and complexes in us. When father makes mother suffer, or mother makes father suffer, or when father and mother are making each other suffer, the seeds of suffering are sown in us and they are watered in our heart. It continues like that, and when the child has grown up he or she carries many painful internal formations and lives with feelings of blame and resentment towards mother, father, or both. When we see ourselves more clearly as a young child who is so vulnerable, we feel sorry for ourselves and we see compassion rising in us and penetrating us. We smile to the five-year-old child with a smile of compassion and love. This is the practice of loving kindness meditation directed towards ourself.

Then, visualize your father or mother as a five-year-old child. Generally, we only see our father as an adult, perhaps a stern and difficult one. However, we know that before he became an adult, he also was a five-year-old child, just as fragile and vulnerable as we were. We see how that young boy cringed, fell silent, and held his tongue whenever his father fell into a thundering rage. We see that young child was the victim of the temper, scowls, and churlishness of his father, our grandfather. If you have a family photograph album, it may be helpful to meditate on a picture of that five-year-old child who was our father or our mother. In our meditation, we have to become acquainted with and smile kindly to that small girl or boy. We have to see his or her fragility and vulnerability, so we will also feel compassion coming up in us. When compassion arises from our heart, we know that our meditation, our looking deeply, has begun to have results. When we can see and understand, then we will be able to love.

Our internal formations will be transformed with this practice. With understanding, we begin to be able to accept. We will be able to use the understanding and the love to return and help our father or mother transform. We know that we can do this because understanding and love have transformed us and we have become more accepting, more gentle, peaceful, and patient.

....

Buddhist Prayers and Gathas

THE FOLLOWING are short Buddhist prayers you can say to yourself throughout the day. You do not have to identify yourself as a Buddhist to use these prayers. They are just small everyday opportunities for anyone to return to the present moment.[11]

Prayers

NOURISHING HAPPINESS

My resources for practice are my own peace and joy.
I vow to cultivate and nourish them with daily
    mindfulness.

---

11 These prayers are collected from *Present Moment, Wonderful Moment* (Berkeley, CA: Parallax Press, 1991) and the *Plum Village Chanting and Recitation Book.*

For my ancestors, family, future generations,
and the whole of humanity, I vow to practice well.

In my society I know that there are countless
  people suffering,
drowned in sensual pleasure, jealousy, and hatred.
I am determined to take care of my own mental
  formations,
to learn the art of deep listening and using loving
  speech
in order to encourage communication and
  understanding
and to be able to accept and love.

Practicing the actions of a bodhisattva,
I vow to look with eyes of love and a heart
  of understanding.
I vow to listen with a clear mind and ears
  of compassion,
bringing peace and joy into the lives of others
to lighten and alleviate the suffering of living beings.

I am aware that ignorance and wrong perceptions
can turn this world into a fiery hell.
I vow to walk always upon the path of
    transformation,
producing understanding and loving kindness.
I will be able to cultivate a garden of awakening.

Although there is birth, sickness, old age, and death,
now that I have a path of practice, I have nothing
    more to fear.
It is a great happiness to live in stability and freedom,
to take part in the work of relieving others' suffering,
the career of Buddhas and bodhisattvas.
In each moment I am filled with deep gratitude.

TURNING TO THE TATHAGATA

We, your spiritual children for countless past lives,
have chased after worldly things,
unable to recognize the clear, pure basis of our
true mind.
Our actions of body, speech, and mind have been
unwholesome.
We have drowned in ignorant cravings, jealousy,
hatred, and anger.
But now the sound of the great bell has caused us
to awaken
with a heart that is determined to renew our body
and our mind.
Please help us completely remove the red dust of all
wrongdoings, mistakes, and faults.

We, your spiritual children in this moment,
make the vow to leave all our habit energies behind,
and for the whole of our life to go for refuge to
the Sangha.
Awakened One, please place your hand over us
in protection,

so that loving kindness and compassion will guide
   and assist us.

May our heart's garden of awakening
bloom with hundreds of flowers.
May we bring the feelings of peace and joy into
   every household.
May we plant wholesome seeds on ten thousand
   paths.
May we never attempt to escape the suffering of
   the world,
always being present wherever beings need our help.
May mountains and rivers be our witness in this
   moment
as we bow our heads and request the Lord of
   Compassion
to embrace us all.

No Coming, No Going

This body is not me.
I am not caught in this body.
I am life without limit.
I have never been born and I never die.

Look at the ocean and the sky filled with stars,
manifestations from my wondrous true mind.

Since beginningless time, I have always been free.
Birth and death are only doors through which we
    pass,
sacred thresholds on our journey.
Birth and death are a game of hide-and-seek.

So laugh with me,
hold my hand,
let us say good-bye,
say good-bye to meet again.

We meet today,
we will meet tomorrow,
we meet at the source in every moment,
we meet each other in all forms of life.

Gathas for Daily Activities

WAKING UP

Waking up this morning, I smile.
Twenty-four brand new hours are before me.
I vow to live fully in each moment
and to look at all beings with eyes of compassion.

LOOKING IN THE MIRROR

Awareness is a mirror
reflecting the four elements.
Beauty is a heart that generates love
and a mind that is open.

TURNING ON THE WATER

Water flows from high in the mountains.
Water runs deep in the Earth.
Miraculously, water comes to us,
and sustains all life.

WASHING HANDS

Water flows over these hands.
May I use them skillfully
to preserve our precious planet.

BRUSHING TEETH

Brushing my teeth and rinsing my mouth,
I vow to speak purely and lovingly.
When my mouth is fragrant with right speech,
a flower blooms in the garden of my heart.

GETTING DRESSED

Putting on these clothes,
I am grateful to those who made them
and to the materials from which they were made.
I wish everyone could have enough to wear.

HUGGING MEDITATION

Breathing in, I am so happy to hug my child.
Breathing out, I know she is real and alive in
 my arms.

SWEEPING

As I carefully sweep the ground of enlightenment,
a tree of understanding springs up from the earth.

CLEANING THE BATHROOM

How wonderful it is to scrub and clean.
Day by day, the heart and mind grow clearer.

WALKING MEDITATION

The mind can go in a thousand directions.
But on this beautiful path, I walk in peace.
With each step, a cool wind blows.
With each step, a flower blooms.

GARDENING

Earth brings us into life
and nourishes us.
Earth takes us back again.
Birth and death are present in every moment.

WASHING VEGETABLES

In these fresh vegetables
I see a green sun.
All dharmas join together
to make life possible.

THROWING OUT THE GARBAGE

In the garbage I see a rose.
In the rose, I see the garbage.
Everything is in transformation.
Even permanence is impermanent.

**PARALLAX
PRESS**

Parallax Press, a nonprofit organization, publishes
books on engaged Buddhism and the practice of
mindfulness by Thich Nhat Hanh and other authors.
For a copy of the catalog, please contact:

Parallax Press
P.O. Box 7355
Berkeley, CA 94707
Tel: (510) 525-0101
www.parallax.org

Monastics and laypeople practice the art of mindful living in the
tradition of Thich Nhat Hanh at retreat communities worldwide. To
reach any of these communities, or for information about individuals
and families joining for a practice period, please contact:

Plum Village
13 Martineau
33580 Dieulivol, France
www.plumvillage.org

Magnolia Grove Monastery
123 Towles Rd.
Batesville, MS 38606
www.magnoliagrovemonastery.org

Blue Cliff Monastery
3 Mindfulness Road
Pine Bush, NY 12566
www.bluecliffmonastery.org

Deer Park Monastery
2499 Melru Lane
Escondido, CA 92026
www.deerparkmonastery.org

The Mindfulness Bell, a journal of the art of mindful living in the tradition of Thich Nhat Hanh, is published three times a year by Plum
Village. To subscribe or to see the worldwide directory of Sanghas,
visit www.mindfulnessbell.org